YEAR C
LENT/EASTER

YEAR C
LENT/EASTER

PREACHING
THE REVISED
COMMON
LECTIONARY

Marion Soards
Thomas Dozeman
Kendall McCabe

ABINGDON PRESS
Nashville

PREACHING THE REVISED COMMON LECTIONARY
Year C: Lent/Easter

This book is printed on recycled, acid-free paper.

Library of Congress Cataloging-in-Publication Data
(Revised for vol. 2)

Soards, Marion L., 1952–
  Preaching the Revised common lectionary : year C.

  Includes Indexes.
  Contents: [1] Advent/Christmas/Epiphany—[2] Lent/Easter.
  1. Lectionary preaching.   2. Bible—Homiletical use.   I. Dozeman, Thomas B.
II. McCabe, Kendall, 1939– .   III. Common lectionary (1992)   IV. Title.
BV4235.L43S63   1994   251   93-30550
ISBN 0-687-33804-2 (v. 1 : alk. paper)
ISBN 0-687-33805-0 (v. 2 : alk. paper)

94 95 96 97 98 99 00 01 02 03 — 10 9 8 7 6 5 4 3 2 1

MANUFACTURED IN THE UNITED STATES OF AMERICA

Contents

CONTENTS

This is one volume in a twelve-volume series. Each volume contains commentary and worship suggestions for a portion of the lectionary cycle A, B, or C. Since the lections for a few special days do not change from one lectionary cycle to another, material for each of these days appears in only one of the volumes. Appropriate cross references in the table of contents lead the reader to material in other volumes of the series.

Introduction

Now pastors and students have a systematic treatment of essential issues of the Christian year and Bible study for worship and proclamation based on the Revised Common Lectionary. Interpretation of the lectionary will separate into three parts: Calendar, Canon, and Celebration. A brief word of introduction will provide helpful guidelines for utilizing this resource in worship through the Christian year.

Calendar. Every season of the Christian year will be introduced with a theological interpretation of its meaning, and how it relates to the overall Christian year. This section will also include specific liturgical suggestions for the season.

Canon. The lectionary passages will be interpreted in terms of their setting, structure, and significance. First, the word *setting* is being used loosely in this commentary to include a range of different contexts in which biblical texts can be interpreted from literary setting to historical or cultic settings. Second, regardless of how the text is approached under the heading of setting, interpretation will always proceed to an analysis of the structure of the text under study. Third, under the heading of significance, central themes and motifs of the passage will be underscored to provide a theological interpretation of the text as a springboard for preaching. Thus interpretation of the lectionary passages will result in the outline on the next page.

Celebration. This section will focus on specific ways of relating the lessons to liturgical acts and/or homiletical options for the day on which they occur. How the texts have been used in the Christian tradition will sometimes be illustrated to stimulate the thinking of preachers and planners of worship services.

I. OLD TESTAMENT TEXTS

A. The Old Testament Lesson

1. *Setting*

2. *Structure*

3. *Significance*

B. Psalm

1. *Setting*

2. *Structure*

3. *Significance*

II. NEW TESTAMENT TEXTS

A. The Epistle

1. *Setting*

2. *Structure*

3. *Significance*

B. The Gospel

1. *Setting*

2. *Structure*

3. *Significance*

Why We Use the Lectionary

Although many denominations have been officially or unofficially using some form of the lectionary for many years, some pastors are still unclear about where it comes from, why some lectionaries differ from denomination to denomination, and why the use of a lectionary is to be preferred to a more random sampling of scripture.

Simply put, the use of a lectionary guarantees a more diverse scriptural diet for God's people, and it can help protect the congregation from the whims and prejudices of the pastor and other worship planners. Faithful use of the lectionary means that preachers must deal with texts they had rather ignore, but about which the congregation may have great concern and interest. The Ascension narrative, which we encounter in this volume as an option for the Seventh Sunday of Easter, might be a case in point. Adherence to the lectionary can be an antidote to that homiletical arrogance that says, "I know what my people need," and in humility acknowledges that the Word of God to be found in scripture may speak to more needs on Sunday morning than we even know exist when we seek to proclaim faithfully the message we have wrestled from the text.

The lectionary may also serve as a resource for liturgical content. The psalm is intended to be a response to the Old Testament lesson, and not read as a lesson itself, but beyond that the lessons may inform the content of prayers of confession, intercession, and petition. Some lessons may be adapted as affirmations of faith, as in *The United Methodist Hymnal,* nos. 887-889; the United Church of Christ's *Hymnal,* nos. 429-430; and the Presbyterian *Worshipbook,* no. 30. The "Celebration" entries for each day will call attention to these opportunities from time to time.

Pastors and preachers in the free-church tradition should think of the lectionary as a primary resource for preaching and worship, but need to remember that the lectionary was made for them and not they for the lectionary. The lectionary may serve as the inspiration for a separate series of lessons and sermons which will include texts not in the present edition, or having chosen one of the lectionary passages as the basis for the day's sermon, the preacher may wish to make an independent choice of the other lessons in order to supplement and illustrate the primary text. The lectionary will be of most value when its use is not a cause for legalism but for inspiration.

As there are no perfect preachers, so there are no perfect lectionaries. The Revised Common Lectionary, upon which this series is based, is the result of the work of many years by the Consultation on Common Texts and is a response to ongoing evaluation of the Common Lectionary (1983) by pastors and scholars from the several participating denominations. The current interest in the lectionary can be traced back to the Second Vatican Council which ordered lectionary revision for the Roman Catholic Church:

> The treasures of the Bible are to be opened up more lavishly, so that richer fare may be provided for the faithful at the table of God's Word. In this way a more representative portion of the holy Scriptures will be read to the people over a set cycle of years. (Walter Abbott, ed., *The Documents of Vatican II* [Piscataway, N.J.: New Century], p. 155)

The example thus set by Roman Catholics inspired Protestants to take more seriously the place of the Bible in their services and sermons, and soon many denominations had issued their own three-year cycles, based generally on the Roman Catholic model but with their own modifications. This explains why some discrepancies and variations appear in different forms of the lectionary. The Revised Common Lectionary (RCL) is an effort to increase agreement among the churches. A table at the end of the volume will list the differences between the RCL and the Roman Catholic, Episcopal, and Lutheran lectionaries. Where no entry is made, all are in agreement with the RCL .

For those unacquainted with the general pattern of the lectionary, a brief word of explanation may be helpful for sermon preparation. (1) The three years are distinguished by one of the Synoptic Gospels: Matthew in A, Mark in B, Luke in C. John is distributed over the three years with a heavy emphasis during Lent and Easter. (2) Two types of readings are used. During the periods of Advent to

Epiphany and Lent to Pentecost, the readings are usually topical—that is, there is some common theme among them. During the Sundays after Epiphany and Pentecost the readings are continuous, with no necessary connection between the lessons. The preacher begins, then, with at least four preaching options: to deal with either one of the lessons on its own or to work with the dialogue between the Old Testament lesson (or Acts in the Sundays of Easter) and the Gospel. Perhaps it should also be added that though the psalm is intended to be a response by the people to the Old Testament lesson—rather than being read as a lesson on its own—this in no way suggests that it cannot be used as the text for the sermon.

This is the second of four volumes that deal with the lessons for Year C of the lectionary. The first volume covered Advent through the time after Epiphany. The third volume will begin with Trinity Sunday (the First Sunday after Pentecost) and will include all the lessons for June, July, and August. The fourth volume will complete the remainder of the year, including the lessons for All Saints' Day (November 1) and Thanksgiving Day.

A note on language: We have used the term *Old Testament* in this series because that is the language employed by the Consultation on Common Texts, at least up to this point. Pastors and worship committees may wish to consider alternative terms such as *First Testament* or *Hebrew Scriptures* that do not imply that those writings somehow have less value than the rest of the Christian Bible. Another option is to refer to *First Lesson* (from the Hebrew Scriptures or from Acts), *Second Lesson* (from Acts or the epistles), and *Gospel.*

THE MIND OF CHRIST IN LENT

Lent is probably the most widely observed season in the Christian year. Churches that ignore Advent, prefer Mother's Day to Pentecost, and isolate the observance of Christmas and Easter to one day each per year are capable of mounting Lenten programs and special emphases on such a scale as to make the Easter sunrise service seem anticlimactic. Religion breaks out all over. The inoculation, in the form of regular church attendance for several weeks, usually works, for by the Sunday after Easter Day, few pietistic eruptions are to be seen remaining on the body ecclesiastical. It seems odd that so much preparation has so little payoff for Christian discipleship.

The purpose of this introduction to Lent is not to provide a different program with a guaranteed long-range payoff, but rather to help those who preach and plan worship think about what they are doing in light of that entire period of time from Ash Wednesday to the Day of Pentecost and to see it as an unbroken chain of days that links us to and makes us one with the apostolic church and its experience of the saving Christ-event.

Remember that Easter Day was originally the only day in the Christian year! The early Christians met weekly on the first day of the week to pray, to break bread, and to share in the apostles' reminiscences of Jesus' earthly ministry (Acts 2:42). Their meetings were characterized by an expectation of their Lord's immediate, sudden return. In this ecstatic atmosphere one did not do long-range planning and goal setting. But even within the pages of the New Testament we have indications that time is fast becoming a threat to Christian faith. Second Peter 3 is an effort to counter the arguments of the scoffers who deride the Christian hope. The answer that in the Lord's sight a thousand years are as one day might help relieve some of the Christian anxiety, but it did not change the fact that the Christians still had to make it through one day at a time on earthly calendars. Time, then, if it was not to be an enemy, had to be made a friend. It was through this domestication of time that the Christian year evolved.

The precise details of the evolution are impossible to know, varying as they doubtless did from region to region. The general outline is rather easy to discern. First, there was the weekly celebration of the Resurrection. This celebration was of the entire Paschal mystery: the Incarnation, the Crucifixion, the Resurrection and Ascension, the gift of the Spirit, and the promise of the Lord's return. There next emerged a special emphasis in the spring on the celebration of the Paschal feast in relation to the actual time of the historical event. This celebration extended itself back through the Crucifixion on Friday and the Last Supper on Thursday, thus creating the Paschal Triduum of Maundy Thursday, Good Friday, and Easter Eve, which carried over into Easter Day. We know that in Jerusalem the custom was begun of having the bishop ride a donkey into the city on the Sunday before the Passion and so inaugurate that period of observance which we call Holy Week. Just as the discrete events leading up to the Resurrection were separated for celebration, so also two other events that had been seen as part of the whole Paschal mystery were also given individual recognition: the Ascension forty days after Easter Day and the anointing by the Holy Spirit at Pentecost fifty days after.

Lent emerged in the form in which we know it today as a combination of the church's catechetical program and penitential discipline. It was catechetical in that it was the final period of intense instruction before the catechumens were brought to the bishop to be baptized at Easter. This was seen as the most appropriate time for baptism, since through that rite the catechumens fully put on Christ by dying and rising with him in the tomb of the font. One cannot overemphasize the interrelationship of baptism and instruction here. The *Apostolic Tradition* of Hippolytus (written around 250 C.E.) indicates that catechumens were to be instructed for three years and that a catechumen who was slain for the faith prior to baptism "will be justified, for he has received baptism in his blood" (chap. 19). The rule seemed to be "no baptism without catechesis." Lent may be a good time to remind ourselves of this principle, not only as we continue the traditional Lenten confirmation classes, but as we also seek to establish classes for parents who will be bringing infants for baptism.

Penitential discipline came to be attached to Lent as the church came increasingly to understand itself as the field where the wheat and the weeds grew together. A major disagreement in the second century had to do with how to deal with those who denied or betrayed the faith during times of persecution. Those of a more rigorous disposition were in favor of excommunication and expulsion with no second chance allowed. The more catholic view prevailed, however, so that those who had sinned were expected to perform appropriate penance and during Lent were finally prepared to be received fully back into the fellowship of the Church during Holy Week, in time to be able to celebrate the Easter mysteries once more with the faithful. It soon became customary for all Christians to use the Lenten period as a time for repentance of past sins and self-denial (hence "giving things up" for Lent), even if their sins had not been of a major or notorious kind.

It is this history which is briefly described in many Ash Wednesday liturgies, such as the following from the *New Handbook of the Christian Year* (p. 112):

> Dear brothers and sisters in Christ: Christians have always observed with great devotion the days of our Lord's passion and resurrection. It became the custom of the church to prepare for Easter by a season of penitence, fasting, and prayer. This season of forty days provided a time in which converts to the faith were prepared for baptism into the body of Christ. It is also the time when persons who had committed serious sins and had been separated from the community of faith were reconciled by penitence and forgiveness, and restored to the fellowship of the church. The whole congregation is thus reminded of the mercy and forgiveness proclaimed in the gospel of Jesus Christ and the need we all have to renew our baptismal faith.

Preachers and planners of worship need, then, to keep in mind these two primary purposes of the Lenten season: the training of candidates for baptism and confirmation, and the encouragement of all the members of the congregation to renew their dedication and commitment.

Lent, then, is not a prolonged meditation upon the Passion and death of Christ, a pre-extended Good Friday. The clue to the meaning of Lent can be found by looking at the two days that frame it, Ash Wednesday and Good Friday. On Ash Wednesday, it is customary in many congregations for persons to have ashes placed upon their heads while they are being told, "Remember that you are dust, and to dust you shall return." In other words, we are confronted by the fact of our mortality in a vivid physical encounter. On Good Friday, we witness the death of another human being, and we are told that in this death we all have died. Lent certainly is intended to end at the cross, but it begins with the human condition that we all share, and it takes on the character of a pilgrimage. The Old Testament lesson for the First Sunday in Lent begins near the end of Israel's pilgrimage through the wilderness as they are called upon to remember God's faithfulness to them through the forty years, and then the epistle calls us to make our own declaration of faith in the saving power of God. The Gospel reading for the First Sunday in Lent is the temptation of Jesus, which occurs at the beginning of his ministry—as he begins his walk toward the cross. All of the readings for Lent provide an opportunity to examine ourselves in relation to the mystery of the cross, to examine ourselves in light of the grace we have obtained through baptism or which we expect to obtain if we are preparing for baptism or confirmation. As we did not celebrate Advent pretending Christmas had not happened, so we do not celebrate Lent as though we know nothing about Easter. Lent is a time of "festive fasting," in the words of Adrian Nocent:

> In the early Christian centuries the faithful thought that [Christ's] return would take place during the night between Holy Saturday and Easter Sunday, since that night was the center of Christian life, being the anniversary of Christ's victory and the moment when that victory became present anew. The fast that marked the Vigil, and indeed the whole Lenten fast, is festive because it is leading up to the victory and return of the Spouse. (*The Liturgical Year 2: Lent,* p. 41)

The traditional color in the West for Lent has been purple, recognizing that we are decorating for the king who is on his way to mount the throne won through the cross. The medieval English use of the "Lenten array" has been increasingly adopted by many churches. This involves the use of unbleached linen for the paraments. Any decorative symbols such as crosses are not embroidered, but are painted, usually in black, red, cream, or some combination of those three. The altar or communion table would be completely covered all around, giving it a coffin-like appearance. Brass or metal altarware would be replaced by a simple cross and candlesticks of wood, or else the cross would be entirely draped in the same kind of unbleached material and tied at the base. The lack of any altar flowers is also appropriate during Lent in preparation for the floral explosion that usually marks the Easter proclamation.

The presentation of the offering can have a seasonal flavor to it by using a response other than the Doxology. During Lent use, for example, the last stanza of "When I Survey the Wondrous Cross":

> Were the whole realm of nature mine,
> that were an offering far too small;
> love so amazing, so divine,
> demands my soul, my life, my all.

The traditional tune is Hamburg, and it reinforces the meditative and introspective mood of the season. When Easter comes, the same text could be used for all of its Sundays but with the traditional tune for the Doxology, Old 100th. Or the tune Rockingham might be used during Eastertide. The text appears to that tune in *The Hymnal 1982* (Episcopal), no. 474; *The Lutheran Book of Worship*, no. 482; *The Mennonite Hymnal*, no. 165; *The Presbyterian Hymnal*, no. 100; and *The United Methodist Hymnal*, no. 299. The text can be found set to both tunes in the last three mentioned hymnals.

First Sunday in Lent

Old Testament Texts

Deuteronomy 26:1-11 provides cultic instructions for the sacrificial offering of first fruits. Psalm 91 is a liturgy to invoke divine protection.

The Lesson: *Deuteronomy 26:1-11*

The Power of Giving

Setting. Deuteronomy 26:1-11 is a liturgical text that describes in detail how the offering of first fruits must be carried out. The text presuppposes a theology of sacrifice. A brief summary of what it means to give within the setting of sacrifice will provide background for interpreting the offering of first fruits. G. Van der Leeuw in his classic study *Religion in Essence and Manifestation* underscores how "giving" within sacrifice is essentially three things: it is personal, it creates communion, and it is reciprocal. First, a personal, sacrificial gift means that the gift is never simply an object of which one is unilaterally disposing, but actually part of one's self. Since the gift is in fact personal (part of one's self) it creates a bond between the giver and the recipient. Second, the gift creates communion because it is an attempt to place one's self in relation to another by means of an object, which when accepted creates a bond between the giver and the receiver. The central point here is to see that the gift is the central force that creates communion (not the giver nor the receiver) because by participating in it both the giver and the receiver are bonded to each other. The communal nature of the sacrificial gift leads to the third conclusion—namely, that the giving of gifts is

19

inherently reciprocal, since both giver and receiver participate in the gift. Van der Leeuw describes the reciprocal nature of sacrificial gifts in the following manner: "Giving demands a gift . . . because the gift allows a stream to flow, which from the moment of giving runs uninterruptedly from doner to recipient and from receiver to giver: 'the recipient is in the power of the giver.' " The gift of the first fruits in Deuteronomy 26:1-11 illustrates these three points.

Structure. Deuteronomy 26:1-11 consists of liturgical instructions that separate into three parts. Verse 1 is essential for interpreting the larger passage, for it provides the setting that is prompting the sacrificial instructions in the first place.

Once Israel has entered the land then the following ritual practice of first fruits must be performed:

    I. The First Ritual Action and Confession (vv. 2-3)
        A. Ritual action (vv. 2-3*a*)
           Take first fruits
           Place it in a basket
           Go to the place (sanctuary)
           Go to the priest
        B. Confession (v. 3*b*)
           Affirmation of being in the land
   II. The Second Ritual Action and Confession (vv. 4-10)
        A. Ritual action (v. 4)
           The priest will take the basket and place it before God
        B. Confession (vv. 5-10)
           A recounting of salvation history in three parts:
             1. Events leading to Egyptian oppression
             2. Events involved in the Exodus
             3. Present situation in the land
  III. The Third Ritual Action (v. 11)
        Worship and communal celebration

Significance. The focus of this text is neither on God nor Israel, but the land. It is the gift and hence the central force that creates a bond between God and Israel. The first task of interpretation is to determine whose gift is the land. Verse 1 answers this question unequivocally. The land is God's gift to Israel. God's ownership of the land and his subsequent gift of it to Israel is the religious basis for the offering of first fruits. The sacrifice is rooted in the confession that the produce of the land, especially the first-ripe fruits, is God's property, which means that it is holy and should be transferred to God.

But the harvest is also Israel's, and this empirical fact provides the starting point for the ritual instructions. Three conclusions follow at this point. First, the offering of first fruits is personal. This is particularly evident in the two confessions that the worshiper is instructed to recite during the liturgical events. These confessions go beyond the simple transfer of the first fruits back to God to include statements about the status of the worshiper in relation to God. In v. 4 the worshiper acknowledges (1) being present in the land and (2) that the offering of first fruits is a sign that God has fulfilled the divine promises of salvation. The historical credo in vv. 5-10 supports the first confession by providing an elaboration of the process by which God brought Israel into the land. Second, the confessions also underscore how the sacrifice creates communion between God and the worshiper. Here we see that the very act of offering first fruits is meant to articulate the relationship between God and Israel that is described briefly in the historical credo. This relationship is rooted in divine promise (v. 3, "the land that the LORD swore to our ancestors to give us."), and it is God's fulfilling of his obligations that is making the ritual possible. Third, the offering of first fruits is reciprocal—so much so, in fact, that it is impossible to decide who is the giver and who is the receiver. If we start at v. 1, with the notice of how God gave Israel the land, then God is the giver and Israel receives the gift through the produce of the land. It then follows that in the offering of first fruits Israel is the receiver giving back the gift. If, however, we start at v. 2, then Israel is the giver and God is the recipient, who returns the gift to the worshiper in v. 11 in the form of the communal feast. This never-ending circle in which the gift of the land is given and received over and over is the primary metaphor of salvation in the book of Deuteronomy, and it gives rise to an ethic, which Van der Leeuw might state in the following way: "I give in order that thou mayest be able to give." When framed in this way, one must expect a blessing from God when giving the divine a gift, not because it is economically in the self-interest of the worshiper, but, simply because that is the way of salvation. The passing back and forth of gifts creates a bond between God and the people of God, with the result that in the end, the principal feature (of giving) is not that someone or other should receive something, but that the stream of life should continue to flow.

The Response: *Psalm 91:1-2, 9-16*

Protection in the Sanctuary

Setting. Psalm 91 is best characterized as a liturgy, because it incorporates a variety of different forms of speech. It begins with an invitation or summons to confession in vv. 1-2, then switches in the next section, when the speaker teaches other worshipers about the protective power of God in vv. 3-13, and, finally, the psalm ends with a divine oracle in vv. 14-16.

Structure. The lectionary has narrowed the scope of the psalm to include the opening summons to confession in vv. 1-2, concluding verses of the teaching section in vv. 9-13, and the divine oracle in vv. 14-16.

Significance. The setting of the psalm is clearly the sanctuary. The imagery of abiding in the shadow of the Almighty (v. 2) and of finding refuge under his wings (v. 4) is language from the cult, where God was envisioned as being enthroned with winged cherubim overhead. The opening invitation is striking and lends itself to liturgical use in a contemporary worship service. It begins with an inclusive "You," but is then immediately qualified by two relative clauses, each of which begins with the word, "who." Those being addressed are the ones who already live under the protection of God, and they are instructed to confess the fact in v. 2: You "will say to the LORD, 'My refuge and my fortress; my God, in whom I trust.'" The confession prompts preaching or teaching in vv. 9-13, most likely by some worship leader. Note the causal sentence in v. 9: "Because you have made the LORD your refuge...." The teaching goes on to underscore how God will in fact protect those who put their trust in him. Then, the psalm actually ends with direct theophany in vv. 14-16, when God confirms the teaching of the worship leader. The language of trust provides important commentary on giving, even though sacrifice is not the topic of the psalm. Note especially the reciprocal nature of the psalm, where it begins with confession by the worshiper and ends with God responding with the promise of protection.

New Testament Texts

On the first Sunday of the season of Lent the lectionary presents two texts seemingly appropriate for this time of reflection and repentance. The reading from Romans in part calls us to confession and faith that signify our salvation, although as examination of the passage shows Paul is not promoting a formula for how to repent in order to be saved. Rather, Paul wrestles with the plight of Israel by thinking about God. The Gospel lesson follows the established pattern for the First Sunday in Lent by directing our attention to the story of Jesus' temptations—now, in Year C, taken from Luke's Gospel. As we shall see Luke provides clues in the account that indicate that he offered this story as an anticipation of Jesus' decisive victory over Satan and evil through the cross, resurrection, and exaltation.

The Epistle: *Romans 10:8b-13*

One Lord of All Humanity

Setting. The lesson comes from Paul's extended and difficult discussion of God's relationship to Israel in the light of the Christ event (Romans 9–11). At the beginning of Romans 10 Paul states that he desires and prays that those Israelites who currently do not believe the gospel of Jesus Christ may be saved (10:1). He continues to speak somewhat favorably of the Israelites through 10:2-3, saying that they are zealous but ignorant, so that they seek to establish their own righteousness rather than to trust God; then, in 10:4 he says, "For Christ is the end of the law so that there may be righteousness for everyone who believes." Both Paul's mixed attitude toward the nonbelieving Israelites and his declaration that Christ has made the law obsolete by bringing righteousness through faith lie behind the verses of this week's lesson.

Structure. The form of argumentation in this lesson may seem strange to modern readers. Paul works from the statements made in 10:1-4, especially in relation to his position that the Israelites ignorantly sought a righteousness of their own rather than the righteousness of God. Some could reply to Paul that scripture directed the Israelites to do exactly what Paul accuses them of doing in error. Thus, Paul engages in a rabbinic style of argument that essentially explains away the literal sense of a text and replaces it with another text. Unfortunately the key text that Paul is "explaining," Leviticus 18:5, is quoted in v. 5 which is not part of our reading. It must be taken into account, however, to comprehend the verses of the epistle reading for this Sunday.

In the reading Paul laces together passages from the Old Testament (v. 8 = Deuteronomy 30:14; v. 11 = Isaiah 28:16 [already quoted more fully and accurately in Romans 9:33]; and v. 13 = Joel 2:32 [3:5 in Hebrew and the Septuagint]). Paul mixes his own comments and perhaps even an early creed (v. 9 or vv. 9-10) with these lines from the Old Testament. The pattern of the argument is "unfolding"; Paul links one line with another by word or thought association. The outcome is that Paul explains the meaning of Leviticus 18:5 so that Joel 2:32 takes its place. The logic and structure is that of ancient Jewish rhetoric, which may turn out to be more helpful in sermon preparation than one initially suspects.

Significance. Above all Paul wants to make the point stated in v. 12, "For there is no distinction between Jew and Greek; the same Lord is Lord of all and is generous to all who call on him." That is the gospel. But Paul knows that it is possible to object to his proclamation on the basis of scripture. Thus, he argues down the potential objection by going himself, and directing the attention of the Romans, to the very passage that could undermine his message. If Paul can use seemingly conflicting parts of the canon of scripture to create a dynamic debate, why can't the preacher do the same today? Congregations may even find it stimulating to recognize difficulties in holy writ. But if this line is chosen, one should proceed with sensitivity and judiciousness—as Paul did.

If scripture says both that "the person who does these things [i.e., the law] will live by them" and that "if you confess with your lips that Jesus is Lord and believe in your heart that God raised him from the dead, you will be saved," what are we to believe? What gives Paul precedence over Moses? We begin by realizing that Paul speaks from the perspective of faith, in the light of the revelation of Christ, and after the cross and resurrection. Paul takes Christ and God's work in Christ as the standard whereby he finds the meaning of sacred texts. Paul does not attribute to Moses the authority of God. What God did and does in Jesus Christ is the final determining factor for how we are to appropriate scripture into our lives. And, in Christ, God acted to do for humanity what we were and will never be able to do for ourselves, God calls us to faith in Jesus Christ. In so doing God establishes the power of his own righteousness in our lives. This act of God means that saving grace runs past ethnic and cultic lines and into the hearts of all humankind. In Christ, God eliminated the kinds of human distinctions that once marked groups off from one another, so that as God in Christ draws us to himself in righteousness, we are drawn to one another in reconciliation. Thus, Paul envisions the meaning of salvation along both vertical and horizontal lines on a universal scale. This is a vision worthy of God.

The Gospel: *Luke 4:1-13*

How to Relate to God

Setting. As we move into the season of Lent we move back in Luke's account of the ministry of Jesus to the story of Jesus' temptation, at the hands of Satan. Luke's version of this moment in Jesus' life is most comparable to Matthew's account of the events (Matthew 4:1-11). Mark only refers to the happenings (1:12-13) and does not narrate the temptation in any detail. Luke differs from both Matthew and Mark by positioning the genealogy of Jesus between the stories of Jesus' baptism and temptation, so that one is not "tempted" in reading Luke to associate these two events. Nevertheless, the story of Jesus' temptation in Luke stands at the beginning of the account of Jesus' ministry as it stands at the beginning of Lent in the lectionary cycle of readings. Thus, as Jesus grappled with doubts at the outset of his ministry, the lesson calls us to face the doubts that hinder our own commitments to God.

Structure. Verses 1-2*a* introduce the story and, then, vv. 2*b*-12 take us through the three-fold temptation of Jesus (vv. 2*b*-4, 5-8, 9-12). Verse 13 brings the story to a conclusion, but in such a way that we anticipate the later overt report of Satan's renewed opposition to Jesus in Luke 22:3.

At first one may focus on the three temptations in an effort to get at the "meaning" of this lesson by reading it as near-allegory. But reflection on the text shows that while there certainly are obvious allegorical elements in the account (recognized at least since the time of Origen!), the nature of Jesus' temptation falls into two categories. Thus, thematically the lesson may be outlined as follows:

I.   The Reality of Temptation
II. The Nature of Temptation
     A. Doubts about identity in relation to God
     B. Doubts about the means to achieving God's ends
        (Both kinds of doubts tempt one away from a
        valid relationship to God.)
III. Temptation Comes and Goes and Comes Again
     (Yet, God is triumphant in Jesus!)

Significance. The similarities between the accounts of Luke and Matthew show that the story of Jesus' temptation was an important memory and point of reflection in many circles of early Christianity. The story is deceptively easy to follow, but certain elements of the narrative invite an interpretation that moves beyond crass literalism. How, for example, could the devil take Jesus to any high place (especially in Palestine!) and show him all the kingdoms of the world in a moment of time? Yet, the apparent symbolic level of the narrative is not permission to run wild with this story as moviemakers are wont to do.

The story is concerned with both Jesus' humanity—he was tempted in all things as are we—and his divine Sonship in relation to God—but without sin. It is also concerned with the means of Jesus' vocation. Through this story we learn the good news that Jesus related to God, despite all difficulties, as God wills for all humanity to relate to God; and in faithfulness to God, Jesus triumphed over evil in such a way that God's ultimate power over all that tempts and oppresses humanity is demonstrated beyond doubt. Indeed, the short notice in v. 13 beckons our minds to the time of Jesus' passion, where he brought God's plan for the salvation of humanity to realization—despite the assembled forces of evil, which sought and seek to thwart God's saving work.

As we follow Jesus through this story, and as he interacts with the devil, we see the temptation to abuse our relationship to God, the temptation to sell out to evil (even for the accomplishment of good), and the temptation to force God's hand as we attempt to be faithful to God's will. To all the devil's devices Jesus responds with lines from Deuteronomy. One of the central concerns of Deuteronomy is full-fledged faithfulness to God despite all adversity. In Jesus we see true love and trust of God. We see all that God does for us and who God calls us to be. Jesus embodies God's will, representing humanity and God, in the relationship to which God calls us—and which, in Jesus Christ, God has made undeniably real.

Lent 1: The Celebration

Confession of faith is paramount in each of today's lessons: the offering of the first fruits in Deuteronomy is accompanied by such a confession ("A wandering Aramean was my ancestor"), Paul stresses the significance of "the word of faith that we proclaim," and Jesus uses statements of faith from Deuteronomy in his battle against temptation. This suggests that use of one of the historic creeds might play a prominent role in today's liturgy. In the early church Lent was the time when catechumens were finally taught the Creed, the Symbol, as it was called, prior to being admitted to baptism. In place of reciting the Creed, its paraphrase, "We Believe in One True God," might be used. (See *The Hymnal* (UCC), no. 5; *The United Methodist Hymnal*, no. 85, and a translation from Martin Luther in the *Lutheran Book of Worship*, no. 374.)

The Deuteronomy lesson makes clear that offering and confession of faith go together. For those churches that begin Lent with the offering of the Lord's Supper, this can be a time for the pastor to help them explore what is involved in this offering. Because people frequently arrive at church to find everything prepared and in place on the table, it is not unnatural for them to assume that the Lord's Supper is being offered to or for them rather than an offering they are making to God. The preacher can help them see that participation in the Supper is an act of confession of faith that is joined to our offering of bread and wine (signs of God's protecting care in nature), which God then graciously gives back to us as memorials of the body and blood of Christ (signs of God's protecting care through eternity). This may be the Sunday to introduce an offertory procession in which the communion elements are presented by members of the congregation.

The theme of confession of faith in all three lessons may also focus in the sermon on the importance of such a confession in our battles with temptation. The confessions in the first two lessons are very specific and personal affirmations of faith; they are not vague sentiments opining that "there must be a God somewhere." Temptation does not assault us in a general way. As we are tempted to specific sins, so we can find help in the specific recalling of how God has acted to stand between us and the power of Satan. We recall Martin Luther bellowing out, "I am baptized!" in order to assert the power of Christ in his life over temptation.

The following Charles Wesley text draws together admirably the themes of offering and confession. It could serve as the sermon or communion hymn for the day.

1. What shall I render to my God
   For all his mercy's store?
   I'll take the gifts he hath bestowed,
   And humbly ask for more.

2. The sacred cup of saving grace
   I will with thanks receive,
   And all his promises embrace,
   And to his glory live.

3. My vows I will to his great name
   Before his people pay,
   And all I have, and all I am,
   Upon his altar lay.

4. The God of all-redeeming grace
   My God I will proclaim,
   Offer the sacrifice of praise,
   And call upon his name.

A strong common meter tune would be most appropriate.

Second Sunday in Lent

Old Testament Texts

Genesis 15 is the story of God's covenant with Abram in which the central concern is the reliability of God. Psalm 27 is a prayer that includes expressions of both confidence and lament.

The Lesson: *Genesis 15:1-12, 17-18*

God and Covenant

Setting. Genesis 15 is about covenant. The chapter is an extended exchange between Yahweh and Abram concerning the latter's lack of progeny (vv. 1-6) and land (vv. 7-21). The chapter presupposes the earlier divine promise of salvation to Abram in Genesis 12:1-3 that he would indeed become the father of a great nation if he followed the call of God by leaving his homeland. The connection to Genesis 12 is important, for we must understand that the Abram of Genesis 15 has become a seasoned traveler in following the call of God, yet he lacks children and land. The problem at the heart of Genesis 15, however, is not the fertility of Abram or his real estate options. Rather the problem of the chapter rests with God. The chapter is raising the question of whether God is reliable to deliver on the promise of salvation.

Structure. As noted Genesis 15 separates into two sections: vv. 1-6 focus on offspring and vv. 7-21 on land or the lack of it. The lectionary has removed a section of divine promise from the reading (vv. 13-16) as well as the list of inhabitants of the land in vv. 19-21.

Significance. The two sections of Genesis 15 are meant to explore the reliability of God. Each section is initiated by a divine speech, which echoes aspects of God's original promise in Genesis 12:1-3. These promises provide the context for Abram to ask some pointed questions of God. Genesis 15:1-6 begins with a vision in which God declares, "Do not be afraid, Abram, I am your shield; your reward shall be very great." But to Abram such promises are beginning to sound hollow. Thus he responds by going to the heart of the matter. What reward can there be if he has no children, at best a distant relative named Eliezer of Damascus may reap some benefit from all of his traveling after divine promises, but it certainly won't be Abram. God immediately responds with the renewed promise of an heir, and we are told in v. 6 that Abram believes God. With Abram now securely anchored in faith, one would think that the story would end. Indeed, if Genesis 15 were Abram's story it probably would have. This chapter, however, is not primarily about Abram or faith. It is about God and whether God is able to deliver on the promise of salvation (e.g., children and land). Given this focus, it is not surprising that it is God who continues the story in v. 7 with another declaration, "I am the LORD who brought you from Ur of the Chaldeans, to give you this land to possess."

The second divine declaration of salvation in v. 7 provides the context for Abram to ask a somewhat different question. Verse 8 does not have the tone of complaint as Abram's earlier response about childlessness had. Nor does the faith of Abram appear to be at issue, because he does not ask how he might believe in the promise. Rather Abram asks an epistemological question about God and God's promises—namely, how he can know that God is reliable. The remainder of Genesis 15 is God's response to Abram's question in v. 8. Thus after Abram prepares the stage for God in vv. 9-12 by splitting a variety of animals, he falls into a trance in v. 12 and, for all practical purposes, leaves the narrative. Two activities of God in vv. 12-17 are meant to illustrate the reliability of God. The first is an oath promise in vv. 13-16 in which God becomes obligated to deliver on the promise of salvation. The second is a ritual in which God, symbolized by a "smoking fire pot," passes through the halved animals. The lectionary reading focuses on this latter act.

The ritual in v. 17 is obscure and most likely the oldest unit of tradition in Genesis 15. Its meaning, however, is at the heart of

31

the chapter, because the ritual is meant to provide an answer to Abram's earlier question of how he can know that God is reliable. A close look at the narrative clarifies certain aspects of the ritual. First, the larger context underscores how this ritual is not a mutual agreement between two parties, because Abram has left the story and is off sleeping. Second, the ritual itself makes clear that a relationship or mystical union (or an ecstatic union) between God and Abram is also not being explored, because God is the only character involved in the action. Third, a comparison to the only other occurrence to such a ritual adds still further insight. In Jeremiah 34:18-20 we learn that the leaders of Judah had gone through such a ritual in taking on certain obligations, and that for them the ritual symbolized a potential curse if they did not live up to their obligations. The curse is that God will make them like "the calf which they cut in two and passed between its parts." When we combine these different pieces of information, then it becomes clear that the ritual in Genesis 15:17 is a divine self-curse should God prove unreliable in giving salvation.

The story is not yet finished. Genesis 15:18a reads, "On that day the LORD made a covenant with Abram." This verse appears to be a later addition to the text, which is meant to provide commentary on the preceding ritual by stating that it signifies covenant. What then does covenant mean for preaching? First, from this text it would appear that covenant does not signify a relationship between Abram and God. Rather it describes divine obligation toward Abram, positively through oath (vv. 13-16) and negatively through self-curse (v. 17). Second, such an understanding of covenant provides insight into God. The story underscores how God is not free, because God has chosen to be in covenant. Third, God's obligation in covenant provides the backdrop for addressing the central question of the chapter—namely, whether the salvific promises of God are reliable. Salvation is reliable precisely because it does not rest on a particular quality of relationship or on some mutual agreement that Abram might establish with God. Instead salvation is secure for no other reason than that God is not free to abandon it.

The Response: *Psalm 27*

A Liturgy Expressing Trust and Petitions

Setting. Psalm 27 exhibits a profound shift in mood, which has prompted some past scholars to argue that Psalm 27 is the combination of two different psalms. A hymn of trust and confidence in vv. 1-6 and an individual lament in vv. 7-14. More recent interpretations have tended to emphasize the unity of the psalm within a liturgical setting.

Structure. The strong shift in mood between vv. 1-6 and vv. 7-14 provides the central clue to the structure of the psalm. But a further distinction is possible between vv. 7-13 and v. 14, since the latter verse is an oracle of salvation that is meant to provide a response to the petitions of vv. 7-13.

Significance. The structure indicates how Psalm 27 is a liturgy that moves in three parts. It begins with confession in vv. 1-6. The content of this section is one of confidence and trust. Yet all references to God are in the third person (e.g., "the LORD" in v. 1 and "he" in v. 5), which gives a formality and distance to the relationship between the psalmist and God. The reference to God shifts to the second person in vv. 7-13 (see, for example, the imperatives, "Hear!" in v. 7 and "Come!" in v. 8, or "your face" in v. 8). Even though the content of pleading and lament is very different in vv. 7-13, the two sections certainly interrelate within the liturgy. It is as though the content of trust from the first section is translated into the syntax of the second section, where the more immediate language of pleading breaks the formality and distance of the earlier third person statements about God in vv. 1-6, and, in so doing, demonstrates trust instead of talking about it. The section of direct pleading to God in the second person gives way to a summary confession of trust in v. 13, where the syntax is more like vv. 1-6. The psalm ends by affirming this liturgical movement of confession to pleading and back to confession by concluding with an oracle of salvation in v. 14. A priest or worship leader responds at the end with the encouragement that the psalmist continue to wait for God.

33

New Testament Texts

The epistle reading presents a swirl of Paul's thought as he addresses the church in Philippi. He urges them to Christ-likeness, away from failed faith; yet, thinking of them in particular, he actually calls for this beloved congregation to continue in the manner of life that is already real among them. The enigmatic text from Luke shows Jesus' security in the face of Herod's hostility; and, moreover, it shows the poise and freedom he possessed in the face of death because of his relationship to God. In the context of Lent both passages point us toward God as the sure source of our hope and security in life and for the future.

The Epistle: *Philippians 3:17–4:1*

Called to Christ in Love and Joy

Setting. The Philippian congregation was the first European church founded by Paul, and it was one with which he maintained a very positive relationship. He was in prison at the time he penned this letter; and he seems to have written for several reasons: (1) to thank the Philippians for their support, physical and spiritual; (2) to discuss Epaphroditus's visit to him in behalf of the Philippians; and (3) to address difficulties and potential problems in the life of the church. The lesson comes at the end of the body of the letter (1:12–3:21) and includes the opening line, a kind of bridge sentence, of the complex parenetic portion of the letter (4:1-20).

In the body of the letter Paul discusses his situation (he was in jail) in 1:12-26, and, then, he issues a series of exhortations, 1:27–2:18. In a similar way, in 2:19–3:1 Paul discusses his plans for the future, and, then, he issues further directions (warnings and admonitions) in 3:2-21 before summarizing his love and will for the congregation in 4:1.

Structure. Through the combination of polemic (vv. 17-19) and declaration (vv. 20-21 + 4:1) Paul instructs the Philippians concerning the character of Christian life. Initially in our reading Paul calls the readers to "imitate" him and others who provide appropriate models for Christian existence (v. 17). As becomes clear from the following lines (vv. 18-19) the Philippians are called away from imitating those who have turned away from the gospel of Christ. Thus, the opening portion of the reading has juxtaposed positive and negative dimensions.

In turn and by contrast, vv. 20-21 are remarkably positive. Paul's highly Christocentric statements are applied to the lives of the Philippians as he declares the future and the hope of Christians whose lives are focused on and in relationship to the "Savior, the Lord Jesus Christ."

In the following verse, 4:1 which opens with "therefore" or "so then," Paul summarizes his position. He declares his love, longing, joy, and pride in relation to the Philippians; then, he instructs them pointedly to stand as they are in the Lord. In all, we find that Paul exhorts, warns, declares, explains, and directs. His aims and angles of approach may help the preacher in thinking about the shape and substance of a sermon on this reading.

Significance. The call to imitation is a call to a positive model and, as we saw, away from a negative pattern. Whatever the general background from which Paul developed this appeal to imitation, we see from his other letters that he thinks in these terms more than once (see, e.g., I Thessalonians 1:6; 2:14). Moreover, we know that he called others to imitate him because he understood himself to live in imitation of Christ (see I Thessalonians 1:6; I Corinthians 11:1). Indeed, in this very letter (2:5-11) Paul has already called the Philippians in a highly dramatic manner to the imitation of Christ.

If the positive value of imitating Christ is not clear, Paul warns against moving in the opposite direction. He recalls those who once lived for the gospel, but who now have not only lost their zeal but apparently have become hostile toward the good news. For the sake of comfort in this life, they have abandoned the costly nature of discipleship which Paul understands to lead to heavenly (eternal) gain. The tone of Paul's remarks at this point are more remorseful than hostile, though he is sternly alerting the Philippians to the peril of apostasy.

Paul does not dwell on the negative. Rather, he joyfully moves to reflect upon the future and the hope of Christians who entrust their lives to their Lord Jesus Christ—that is, to their Savior who in the power of his resurrection and exaltation has begun and continues to transform their lives as he establishes his rule of cosmic hegemony. Even here, however, as Paul moves into the stratosphere of christological reflection, he does not lose contact with reality. As he thinks about the Philippians he speaks of his love, his desire to be with them, his joy over them, and his pride in their life as a community of faith. With such thoughts in mind, Paul simply tells the Philippians to "keep on keeping on"—that is, they are to live all the more in the way that they have been living—in faithful relation to their Lord and Savior Jesus Christ.

The Gospel: *Luke 13:31-35*

The Security of Devotion to God

Setting. As Jesus makes his journey to Jerusalem, where he infers he will die, he teaches, heals, and confronts adversaries along the way. Here, remarkably, the Pharisees with whom Jesus is most often in dispute come to him and warn against any confrontation with Herod (Agrippa) who has clear negative intentions toward Jesus. The passage gives us the Pharisees' warning and Jesus' reply. The incident and statement in vv. 31-33 are unique in the New Testament, whereas the words of Jesus recorded in vv. 34-35 find a striking parallel (well worth comparing) at Matthew 23:37-39.

Structure. The text falls into two related parts: First, in vv. 31-33 the Pharisees come to Jesus warning him of the danger related to Herod Agrippa, and he replies to them. At the end of his response we find a reference to Jerusalem that provides the basis of the ensuing statements in vv. 34-35, which reveal Jesus' concern for Jerusalem and his perception of the city's fate.

Within the major sections of the passage are facets that are suggestive for preaching. First, we see Jesus pointing to the ultimate powerlessness of human opposition to God's will. Second, Jesus states his own unswerving commitment to God's will at all costs. Third, Jesus' declarations point to the overarching divine necessity that ultimately determines the outcome of events. And, fourth, Jesus' prophetic lament and revelatory declaration demonstrate the terrible plight of humanity set in opposition to the will of God.

Significance. This lesson is indeed difficult for us today, for it presents a worldview that is very different from our own post-Enlightenment (now, post-Modern) assumptions about reality. We typically assume that humans are essentially free, even autonomous, individuals—although contemporary social theory has taught us that we are inescapably connected to the larger complexes of community and society around us. We also understand history to be a system that basically operates in terms of cause-and-effect—although we do allow for "chance" and "chaos" putting odd twists on the way in which life unfolds. Jesus' words, however, refer to the ultimate powerlessness of persons and the ultimate authority of God, which finally determines the course of life.

What are we to make of Jesus' statements? In preaching, one must deal with the tensions between the worldview of the text and the worldview that we inherit in our own age. It will not do simply to ignore the one or the other, and it will not prove satisfactory to denounce one perspective and to advocate the other. The text calls us to think about God, the world, and ourselves in a manner that relates God, world, and ourselves in a thorough and vital fashion. In the mix, the text also calls us simultaneously to let God be God, not merely a misty "other," and to take seriously our responsibility in relation to God's will.

Jesus' words reveal that God has a definite will for the course of life in this world. The statements also recognize that while humans are finally unable to thwart God's will, we humans can indeed resist God, bringing ourselves into peril because we are set against divine reality which moves toward God's purposes in the world, despite our opposition. In this scheme of things, two items merit attention. First, we should recognize that the will and work of God of which Jesus speaks are the will and work for our salvation—that is, God is at work for our well-being. God is not merely exercising brute force, doing what God wants simply to get God's own way. God is neither an immature child nor a ruthless despot. The larger story of Jesus' life, work, death, resurrection, and exaltation coheres to inform us who God is and what it is that God wills and works for. Second, Jesus himself reveals the manner in which we are to relate to God. Jesus declares and demonstrates unswerving devotion to doing

God's will despite all costs. Jesus himself shows us what it means to be freed from paralyzing fear by the security that comes through commitment to God. The security that Jesus knew and to which we are called is the certitude that God is able to sustain us in our relationship to God no matter what forces arise against us in this world. As we "let God be God" and as we devote ourselves to doing God's will, we find the freedom that allows us to live without fear and into the fullness of life that God intends for us.

Lent 2: The Celebration

Having been told on p. 11 that during the period from Ash Wednesday through the Day of Pentecost there will usually be a thematic connection between the lessons, the reader may begin to experience a kind of quiet desperation after seeking for such a connection today. The reason for that is because the first two lessons were assigned originally in the Roman Catholic lectionary to accompany the Gospel lesson of the Transfiguration, which in the Roman Catholic calendar is observed on the Second Sunday in Lent. The Common Calendar observes the Transfiguration on the Last Sunday after Epiphany, two weeks earlier, but the Revised Common Lectionary transferred only the Gospel reading to that day and not the whole set of lessons. Understanding that the Gospel reading is the Transfiguration, then it makes sense to have the Old Testament reading describing a theophany in which God reveals the future, and an epistle reading that describes how we will participate in Christ's glory. As it is, the preacher today is left with three very different lessons and is advised to work with only one of them. An imaginative sermon could conceivably play off the images of the promised land (Genesis), the city that slays the prophets (Luke), and the heavenly citizenship (Philippians) in which both are realized and redeemed. One must beware, however, of anti-Semitic overtones and instead contemporize the texts so that it is we who are caught between the hope of the promise and the reality of that sinfulness, which can only be overcome by the faithfulness of God in Christ who makes the heavenly identity possible. Such an approach calls for a poetic rendering of images rather than a deductive explication of texts.

The last line in the Gospel reading is the liturgical formula that occurs at the end of the Eucharistic sanctus in some liturgies: "Blessed is [he] the one who comes in the name of the Lord." It will be repeated in Luke's Gospel on Passion/Palm Sunday in the story of the triumphal entry into Jerusalem. Just as, in spite (or because) of the sin of Jerusalem, Jesus kept his divine appointment, so our sin does not deter the Lord's presence in the Eucharist. Rather, we can depend upon God's faithfulness to come bringing forgiveness and reconciliation. This may be good news to those who have been raised with perfectionist ideas about "not being good enough to take communion."

The African American spiritual, "City Called Heaven," will provide an appropriate musical bridge between the epistle and Gospel readings or a response to the epistle reading alone. It can be found in *Songs of Zion* (Nashville: Abingdon Press, 1981), no. 135.

Third Sunday in Lent

Old Testament Texts

Isaiah 55:1-9 is a divine announcement of salvation, which emphasizes the presence of God in the midst of exile. Psalm 63:1-8 is a prayer expressing trust in God during times of threat.

The Lesson: *Isaiah 55:1-9*

God's Thoughts and Ways

Setting. Isaiah 55 provides the epilogue to the message of Second Isaiah. In interpreting Isaiah 55, therefore, keep in mind that we are reading a conclusion that has incorporated themes and motifs introduced in chapter 40 and developed throughout Isaiah 40–55. The prophet was called in chapter 40 to proclaim a word of comfort and salvation to exilic Israel. In 40:6-11 of the prophet's call there was an exchange, where Second Isaiah expressed doubt (vv. 6-7) about God's ability to save. This doubt was stated through the metaphor that life was like grass, which is here today and gone tomorrow. The divine response to the prophet's doubt is stated in v. 8 with the following words: "The grass withers, the flower fades; but the word (Hebrew, *dabar*) of our God will stand forever" (Hebrew, *'olam*). The call of Second Isaiah then ends with the imagery of God feeding Israel as though the divine were a shepherd and Israel a flock of sheep (v. 11). Isaiah 55 closes the message of Second Isaiah by returning to all of these motifs. It begins with the divine invitation for Israel to eat freely (vv. 1-3*a*). Then Israel is reminded that there are divine promises which last forever (vv. 3*b*-5). Finally, the chapter closes by returning to the topic of God's word (v. 11).

Structure. Past form-critical studies have underscored how chapter 55 might be separated into two or three smaller units consisting of vv. 1-5, 6-13 (or 9-11 and 12-13). More recent studies have questioned any reading of Isaiah 55 that would separate too strongly the smaller units of the chapter as though they were meant to function as independent units. In either case, whether we emphasize the smaller units or the chapter as a whole, vv. 1-9 do not present a natural unit within the chapter. The problems with the boundaries of the lectionary reading go beyond style, because a reading of Isaiah 55 that ends at v. 9 ("For as the heavens are higher than the earth, so are my ways higher than your ways, and my thoughts than your thoughts.") encourages an interpretation that emphasizes how God is removed from humans, when, in fact, the message of the prophet is just the reverse: that God is surprisingly close to exilic Israel. Isaiah 55 can be outlined in three sections: first, a call to drink and eat freely (vv. 1-3*a*) and the reasons for it (vv. 3*b*-5); second, a call to seek God while he is near (vv. 6-7) and the reasons for doing so (vv. 8-11); and, third, the inevitable results (vv. 12-13).

Significance. Two questions are central for preaching this text. What is the good food that God is freely offering exilic Israel (v. 2)? And what is hindering them from eating it?

What is the good food? Verses 1-5 introduce the first question with mixed metaphors in vv. 1-3*a*. The text begins with an offer to drink water then it shifts to an offer of food. But both metaphors eventually give way in vv. 2*b*-3*a* to the motif of hearing (Hebrew, *sama'*). Upon first reading, it appears that the strong call to hear in v. 2*b* ("Listen carefully to me") is meant to call attention to the next line, which is an offering to eat good food ("eat what is good"). As we read on in v. 3*b*, however, the metaphor of food gives way completely to the motif of hearing ("Incline your ear, and come to me; listen [Hebrew, *sama'*] so that you may live."). This shift from eating to hearing suggests that divine speech is the free food from God. Verses 3*b*-5 support this conclusion by introducing God's everlasting covenant with David. This covenant of unending support and care for the people of God is free food for Israel, which cannot run out, because God is obligated to keep cooking.

What is hindering Israel from eating the food? The answer simply put is the Exile. As a conquered and deported nation living on the edges of the Babylonian empire, exilic Israel does not even know where God's dining room is, much less whether there is any food on a table within it. Verses 6-13 explore this problem through the spatial metaphor of whether God is distant or near. Verse 6 presents the central message of this unit that God is very near to exilic Israel. In the context of Isaiah 55, the "wicked thoughts and ways" that must be abandoned in v. 7 are best interpreted as the seemingly natural conclusion that God is in fact very distant and removed from exilic Israel. The remainder of the text presents four arguments in vv. 8, 9, 10-11, and 12-13 to support the claim of divine nearness. Each of these arguments is introduced with the word "for" (Hebrew, *ki*). Verse 8 underscores the contrast between God and exilic Israel, while v. 9 expands the contrast by introducing the spatial metaphor of heaven and earth. Verses 10-11 build on the contrast that has been created in vv. 8 and 9 to provide the central message. God may seem distant upon first instinct to exilic Israel, but, in fact, God's word (Hebrew, *dabar*) is all around them, like rain and snow that saturates the earth. And like these natural elements, the divine word will inevitably nourish those upon whom it has fallen. Verses 12-13 sketch out the inevitable results of God's nearness to Israel. Israel will return from exile.

In summary, two points are central for preaching this text. First, the text is meant to evaluate critically our tendency to make conclusions about divine activity based on our circumstances. This point is achieved by the strong contrast in vv. 8 and 9. Our thoughts are not God's thoughts. God is in heaven, and we are on earth. Second, the contrast is not meant to belittle humans over against a majestic God, but to underscore the value of humans to God. This second point requires that the entire chapter be read. If the text ends at v. 9 (as the lectionary reading suggests), then the message is that God is, in fact, removed from exilic Israel to the point where God has left the world altogether. Such an interpretation makes no sense of the proclamation of divine nearness in v. 6 and actually supports the "wicked thoughts and ways" that are being rejected in the divine speech. The free food of God is the divine word that is always present like rain in soil. This revelation is what prompted the prophetic career of Second Isaiah in the first place (40:8).

The Response: *Psalm 63:1-8*

A Psalm of Confidence

Setting. Psalm 63 is a psalm of trust or confidence that presupposes the setting of the sanctuary. Verses 9-11 give some indication that the psalm was used during times of threat.

Structure. Psalm 63 separates into two parts: vv. 1-4 indicate a situation of need but are dominated by language of trust; vv. 5-8 explore in even more detail the confidence of the singer in God's ability to help.

Significance. Psalm 63 provides an excellent response to the Old Testament lesson. The lectionary removes the ending of the psalm, which underscores how the singer is in a threatening situation. This need not present a problem when the psalm is used as a response to Isaiah 55, since this text has already sketched out the threatening situation of the exile. The imagery of thirst in v. 1 along with the confession that God's steadfast love gives life in v. 3 corresponds well with the offer of free water in Isaiah 55:1. The analogy in imagery to Isaiah 55 continues in the second section where thoughts of God are equated with a feast in vv. 5-6.

New Testament Texts

Both readings are warnings against spiritual self-contentment that leads to a presumptuous attitude toward God's grace. Both readings warn against assuming one's spiritual superiority in relation to others. Both passages remind us starkly that God holds final authority and has final say in evaluating us. And both texts end in such a manner that we recognize that we have hope in relation to God even if at present we are in a perilous position.

The Epistle: *I Corinthians 10:1-13*

The Lesson of Israel in the Wilderness for Us Today

Setting. We first encountered I Corinthians in Year C in the readings for the Second Sunday After the Epiphany, and the following remarks about setting repeat, in part, the observations made earlier.

43

Paul's letter to the Corinthians treats an amazing variety of concerns, all of which are related to the desire of the members of the church to boast of their spiritual superiority. As Paul portrays the situation, spiritual arrogance is tearing apart the body of Christ as one faction and then another parades its spirituality. Paul's letter shows that he understands all this inappropriate behavior to be nothing more than destructive boasting.

Our epistle reading comes in the section of the body of the letter that runs from I Corinthians 5:1–11:1. From I Corinthians 7:1, 25; 8:1; 12:1; and 16:1 we can see that Paul is often replying to a letter the Corinthians sent to him to inquire about their situation. In dealing with the problem of boasting Paul forms a series of vivid arguments. Our reading is a loose "midrash" on events in Exodus and Numbers, which is designed to warn against the artificial security of self-perceived spirituality. In the context of Lent, the passage should call us to examine our spiritual self-perception and relationship to God.

Structure. There are three broad movements to the reading. First, vv. 1-4 tell the story of Israel's experience in the wilderness in order to draw analogies to the life of the church. In vv. 1-2 Paul writes of Israel's passing through the sea in such a way that one thinks of the Christian experience of baptism; and, then, in vv. 3-4 Paul recalls Israel's partaking of divinely provided food and drink, a parallel experience to partaking of the Lord's Supper. Second, v. 5 issues a blunt, shocking warning: Despite Israel's benefits from God in the wilderness, God was displeased and struck them down! Third, vv. 6-13 interpret and apply the already clear lesson, reinforcing Paul's point. In this section v. 9 states the problem overtly—the Corinthians are, or are in danger of, testing God. Verse 11 recognizes the charged eschatological moment in which the Corinthians stand. Everything in vv. 6-12 functions as a warning, and v. 13 completes Paul's thinking and teaching by calling the Corinthians back to God and away from the deception of self-sufficiency. The movement of the epistle reading is from lesson to warning to elaboration of the situation to call and assurance. The dynamic of the text may well inform the structure and the content of the sermon.

Significance. The problem Paul perceives in Corinth, where the members of the church are preoccupied with their own spirituality, is that the Corinthians are "testing God"—that is, the members of the congregation are so self-contented because of their spiritual gifts, experiences, and practices that they are ignoring God. The focus on the gifts rather than the Giver causes the Corinthians to be puffed up with pride rather than to be thankful to God. The Corinthians are taking God for granted. They bask in the warm glow of grace rather than live faithfully in grateful reception of God's good gifts. The mentality is this: Jesus did it, come and get it; and once you get it, it's all yours!

Paul warns against this kind of thinking and living by telling the story of Israel (vv. 1-4) and by reminding the Corinthians that God determines the moment in which they now stand (v. 11). The good things of God that the Israelites received in the wilderness did not give them special status. When they took God's graciousness for granted, enjoying the gifts and ignoring the Giver, God did not tolerate their misbehavior. And so, Paul tells the Corinthians (and us) that there is no magic in baptism and the Eucharist. We do not take God's grace to go our own ways and all the while be guarded against God's judgment of our own misdeeds. The Corinthians stood and we stand at the juncture of the ages. Through the work of God in Jesus Christ the present, corrupted structures of the world are passing away and the new, God-given patterns of life and relationships to God and to one another are coming into existence. The transformation of reality is the work of God, and we are to be caught up in God's grace, but not to presume upon it.

The solution to human presumptuousness, in relation to the gracious work of God, is God. As Paul says, "God is faithful and he will not let you be tested beyond your strength, but with the testing he will also provide the way out so that you may be able to endure it." Rather than to test God, Paul says we are to trust God so that as we live, we do not depend upon our special spiritual status, but we always have faith in God—because God is faithful!

The Gospel: *Luke 13:1-9*

What Now Shall We Do?

Setting. Luke presents a collection of Jesus' teachings to his disciples and to the throngs that followed him in 12:1–13:9. This section

45

of the Gospel is a subsection of the first major section of Jesus' teaching on discipleship and ministry (9:51–13:21) in the portion of the Gospel that narrates the doings and sayings of Jesus on the way to Jerusalem (9:51–19:27). In this lesson the materials in 13:1-5 are without parallel in the other Gospels, but the parable in 13:6-9 finds a kind of loose parallel in the story of Jesus' cursing of the fig tree, which is told in both Matthew (21:18-20) and Mark (11:12-14, 20-21).

In the context of Lent the "sense" of the story and parable are clear. The story warns against presumed spiritual security, and the parable warns against a fruitless existence in the light of God's grace given to us.

Structure. There are three sections to the lesson, vv. 1-3, 4-5, 6-9. The first two portions of the text issue and reinforce the same warning: Don't assume all is well merely because the misfortunes of others are not visited upon you; your peril is equally great! Then, the parable shows that the grace of God comes to us with expectation of results. Implicit in the parable is a note of hope, not merely the threat of judgment. The "logic" of the lesson is suggestive for preaching: (1) Don't take comfort in the misfortunes of others; (2) Peril is real and universal among sinful humans; (3) God is gracious, and God expects grace to evoke results; and (4) In the face of God's judgment, we are given, by God's grace, yet another chance. Seeing this pattern of thought, one cannot help asking, "What now shall we do?"

Significance. The opening report of the murder by Pilate of the Galileans who were offering sacrifices seems to be a neutral report, but the response of Jesus lets us know that those bearing the news assumed a quid pro quo system of divine reward and retribution— that is, those slaughtered got what they deserved. Jesus rejects this interpretation. He tells the people bluntly that humans are sinners, and that from God's perspective the peril is equal. We cannot evaluate the spiritual condition of others (or ourselves) because we (or they) do or do not suffer. Jesus stands the seeming sign of assurance on its head and calls for those who bore the news, for those who did not suffer and who seemingly assume that they are in God's good graces, to repent. In referring to the death of those upon whom a tower fell, Jesus reinforces the point. Humans need to look to God, not to themselves and their life experiences, for the security for living.

In turn, the warning against fruitlessness in the parable of the fig tree is not a recast call to so-called "works righteousness," and it does not suggest that we maintain our relationship to God by virtue of our own achievements. Rather, in a striking way, the parable reminds us that whatever good we experience comes to us by the grace of God. In giving us grace, God has purpose: we are to be "fruitful"—that is, our lives are to take on the characteristics that God intends. When we live taking advantage of God's many graces, yet bearing no fruit—that is, living simply for ourselves with no observable benefit for God and others—God is displeased. But while displeasure may be real, we have the comforting assurance of God's giving us "room to grow and produce." The final word of this lesson is a call to experience and be transformed by God's grace. The plain news is this: It does make a difference how we live. God cares, and God evaluates our lives—though not in ways that are overtly perceptible to us. We must take stock of our situation, and if we are out of kilter with God's will we are to understand that God expects us to change; and God is at work in our lives to effect the desired change. The message is ultimately good news with real implications for our lives, the question is, "What now shall we do?"

Lent 3: The Celebration

The theme echoing through the lessons today is the conversion of the Church, in the face of constant threat or present exile. Such conversion is not to be understood in absolutist terms, as though church members are consigned to damnation until they have duplicated someone else's experience and after that they are home free. The conversion referred to here is better understood as a Christian lifestyle, an attitude of continually turning toward God in repentance. It is what Luther had in mind when he spoke of the Church as reformed and always reforming. We can never rest on our laurels, whether they be understood to be a particular kind of conversion "experience," active involvement in programs of social concern, or participation in sacramental and liturgical forms that we find personally satisfying and fulfilling. All of these can assume the character of idolatry by becoming ends in themselves toward which we want others to bow in order to reinforce the validity of our own experience.

Penance is the term the Church has used over the centuries to describe this attitude of interior, ongoing conversion. In the Roman Catholic Church it has frequently taken the form of private auricular confession; latterly there has been a movement towards congregational confession and "reconciliation rooms," which resemble a pastoral counseling office more than the confessional box. Most Protestants have maintained some form of public confession of sin in their services, and for many the annual revival service has taken on a sacramental aspect as a time to recommit oneself to Christ.

Today's liturgy may be constructed to provide an opportunity for the community to demonstrate its repentance by appropriate acts of contrition. Remember that the lessons are addressed to communities, not individuals, so phrase the acts of worship in plural forms.

On the basis of the considerations mentioned in the Old Testament exegesis above, that lesson might be expanded to include the whole chapter. Verses 6 and 7 may also be used as a call to worship or as the words of assurance after the prayer of confession. Two contemporary hymns based on Isaiah 55 have recently appeared. One or more stanzas might be used by a solo voice as a response to the lesson or between the prayer of confession and the words of assurance. In *The Hymnal: A Worship Book* (Church of the Brethren and Mennonite) is "O Let All Who Thirst" (no. 495), and in *The United Methodist Hymnal* is "Come, All of You" (no. 350).

Fourth Sunday in Lent

Old Testament Texts

Joshua 5:9-12 describes the Israelites' first actions after they enter the promised land of Canaan. Psalm 32 is a song about salvation.

The Lesson: *Joshua 5:9-12*

Ending the Trip

Setting. Joshua 5:9-12 is a deuteronomistic text. Scholars use this term to refer to one of the dominant voices in the formation of the Old Testament. The voice of these writers is most clear in the book of Deuteronomy. The language, style, and theology of Deuteronomy provide evidence to see the influence of these writers both after the book of Deuteronomy in Joshua through Kings (the Former Prophets also referred to as the deuteronomistic history) and prior to it in Genesis through Numbers (the first four books of the Pentateuch). The literary outline of the deuteronomistic account of the Pentateuch and the Former Prophets is very much a matter of debate among biblical scholars, and the reader is encouraged to pursue this research elsewhere for more detailed discussion. One aspect of the larger context of deuteronomistic writing in the Pentateuch is important, however, for interpreting the Old Testament lesson. It is the parallel between Israel's salvation from Egypt in the book of Exodus and their entrance into the land of Canaan.

In the deuteronomistic account, Israel's salvation is framed by two bodies of water, the Red Sea and the Jordan River, both of which are crossed by Israel on dry ground. The repetition suggests that salvation is inaugurated by the event at the Red Sea for the deuteronomistic writers and that it is meant to come to a conclusion when Israel passes through the Jordan River. This large parallel provides the setting for other repetitions. The rite of circumcision recalls the incident of Moses and Gershom in Exodus 4, while Passover links the narrative back to Exodus 12. The repetitions underscore how salvation is not a single event for the deuteronomistic writers. Rather they conceive of salvation as a physical and spiritual journey, and, because of this, geography is far more than a simple recounting of a past migration. It actually becomes a metaphor for salvation—the hell of slavery in Egypt and the heaven of Canaan are linked by the journey through the wilderness, which is framed by the two bodies of water. The deuteronomistic writer's large vision of salvation as a journey from Egypt to Canaan will provide the starting point for interpreting Joshua 5:9-12.

Structure. Although Joshua 5:9-12 is a short text, it is hardly a simple one. These few verses lace together many of the central cultic acts of worship in ancient Israel. Verse 9 gives a reason for the name Gilgal, which is meant to provide a conclusion to the account of circumcision in vv. 2-8. Since this verse is not meant to stand alone, nor meant to begin a section, the reader may wish to expand the text to include aspects of the previous account of circumcision. Verses 10-12 link together the celebration of Passover, the ceasing of manna, and the beginning of the land as the source of Israel's nourishment.

Significance. When the larger framework of the deuteronomistic story of salvation is brought to light—the trek between the two waters—then it becomes clear that Joshua 5:9-12 is a story about realized salvation. The Jordan River has already been crossed in the previous chapter and Israel is now encamped in the promised land of Canaan. Two motifs in the story are meant to underscore this point. The first is the divine speech to Joshua in v. 9 with its emphasis on the present moment as the fulfillment of salvation that was only begun with the Exodus, "Today I have rolled away from you the disgrace of Egypt." The second is the ceasing of manna in v. 12, which symbolized divine care during the in-between-time of the wilderness journey. When vv. 9 and 12 are read together they state that both the inauguration of salvation (the Exodus) and the intermediate time of journey (the wilderness) are now complete. Joshua 5:9-12 is about realized salvation in the land of Canaan.

How do the people of God live in the heaven of Canaan when the journey is over? Two rituals take center stage: circumcision and Passover. The account of circumcision in vv. 2-9 provides at least two interpretations of the event. The first in vv. 2-8 centers on the name Hill of Foreskins in v. 3. In this account it is explained that all the males were circumcised because the first generation (those previously circumcised in Egypt) died on the journey. A second interpretation is added in v. 9 by shifting the focus from the Hill of Foreskins to Gilgal. The imaginative meaning of the word play between "I have rolled away (Hebrew, *galal*) the reproach of Egypt" and the place name Gilgal is not exactly clear. At the very least, however, Gilgal and the rite of circumcision are meant to signify the end of the journey that started in Egypt, and that the ending of the journey is God's doing (note the first person divine speech). The rite of circumcision prepares the community for Passover at Gilgal, which becomes the point of focus in vv. 10-12. The ritual of Passover is not explained in the text. Instead it is associated with the ceasing of manna and Israel's eating the fruit of the land. (See the commentary for Holy Thursday, Year C, Lent/Easter, and a discussion of Passover.)

Two points are important for preaching this text. Both have to do with the setting and larger literary context of the story. The first point is the setting of worship at Gilgal as the location where the story of salvation ends. Worship signifies the realization of salvation and not a wilderness journey. Another way to say this is that worship is the end of the story of salvation, it is the place where the people of God commune directly with God and not indirectly through manna in the wilderness. The ritual means for communion is the central sacramental rites of circumcision and Passover, and here the preacher may wish to explore how circumcision and Passover at Gilgal are the forerunners to Baptism and Eucharist in Christian tradition.

The second point concerns the militarism that predominates in the book of Joshua, which frequently causes uneasiness in modern readers. The larger context of the deuteronomistic story of salvation is important for addressing this point. Even though the book is certainly about conquest at any cost, the militarism is more about holy war than nationalism. This distinction is important. Joshua 5:9-12 has underscored how salvation is over for Israel at the outset of the book, and that it was God's doing (see v. 9). Conquest stories only begin in the next chapter with Jericho. Joshua 5:9-12 makes it clear that conquest is not salvation to the deuteronomistic writers. If it were, then the Jordan River crossing should occur at the close of the book of Joshua, rather than at the opening. Instead, conquest becomes a motif for describing God's reclaiming of his land. Israel's participation in God's holy war to reclaim the land is rooted primarily in cultic or worship activity. Joshua 5:9-12 has emphasized how Israel must purify themselves in worship in order to see the hand of God outside of worship, and that this action must be the source for acquiring courage to participate in God's mission. The cultic rituals that describe Israel marching around the city of Jericho underscore this latter point. Note how the walls of Jericho simply fall down because of divine activity. The deuteronomistic writers are certainly not passivistic, but their primary point in the conquest stories is less the slaughter of the Canaanites and more the presence or absence of courage in the Israelites to follow God at any cost. Such courage is possible for the deuteronomistic writers because, for all practical purposes, the central battles of salvation were already over when Israel crossed the Jordan and worshiped God at Gilgal.

The Response: *Psalm 32*

A Song of Thanksgiving

Setting. Psalm 32 is difficult to classify. While it includes aspects of wisdom in vv. 1-2, it also has a section in which the psalmist confesses sin, and it closes with thanksgiving.

Structure. The psalm goes through a number of shifts in mood and speakers. It begins in vv. 1-2 with a tone of wisdom in describing the happy state of those forgiven by God, in vv. 3-5, the psalmist moves to biography to recount a past experience of sin, and in vv. 6-7 offer insight into divine forgiveness, that it might provide security. Verses 8-9 shift to teaching or didactic wisdom, either of the psalmist to other worshipers or of God to the psalmist, and the psalm ends with a summary exclamation of praise in vv. 10-11.

Significance. Hans-Joachim Kraus's comments in *Psalms 1–59: A Commentary* (Minneapolis: Augsburg Fortress, 1988 [p. 372]) provide a direct point of contact between Psalm 32 and Joshua 5:9-12: "The secret of Psalm 32 . . . lies in the fact that this song from the very beginning takes the hearer and reader into the cheering reality of forgiveness and the bestowal of salvation." The point of his comment is that Psalm 32 must be read from the perspective of someone who has fully experienced the salvation of God and not from the point of view of someone who is looking for it. This is also the point of view of Joshua 5:9-12, which makes Psalm 32 an appropriate response to the Old Testament lesson.

New Testament Texts

Two memorable and beloved passages form the New Testament readings for this Sunday. Paul's often-quoted statement concerning "a new creation" stands in the lines from II Corinthians 5 amidst poetically beautiful and enigmatic statements about the saving work of God in Jesus Christ. In turn, the Gospel lesson presents one of the best-known parables, the one usually called "the prodigal son." Both texts are powerful declarations about the grace and grandeur of God, especially as we know God in and through Jesus Christ.

The Epistle: *II Corinthians 5:16-21*

The Heart of the Gospel

Setting. We first encountered II Corinthians in Year C on the Last Sunday After Epiphany, so that the following remarks on setting repeat previous comments.

The situation behind the writing of II Corinthians is very different from that which led to the composition of I Corinthians. Sometime after Paul wrote I Corinthians, a group of outsiders arrived in Corinth. These preachers claimed to possess extraordinary power;

indeed, they maintained that they were sources of divine power. Paul designates these people as "super-apostles."

There are very distinct sections in II Corinthians, which vary greatly in concern and tone. The section of II Corinthians from 2:14–6:13 (or 7:4) is an impassioned plea with the Corinthians in which Paul explains that the character of his ministry is consistent with the character of the gospel. Within II Corinthians 2:14–7:4 we find that 3:7–5:21 is a discussion of the appropriateness of the substance and style of Paul's ministry. The verses of our reading come at the end of this discussion. In reading this passage it is important to recall that Paul is responding to criticism from both the so-called "super-apostles" and some members of the Corinthian congregation.

Structure. Paul's argument simply unfolds. He says that he once knew Christ according to the flesh, meaning by that strange sounding phrase that he had once judged Jesus according to the standards of this world. Then, he insists that he no longer knows Christ in this way. Clearly, Paul means to signal the reality of change; and so, he begins to talk of "new creation" and the dramatic alteration of life in relation to God's work in Christ. Next, Paul declares, "All this is from God!" And, then, he unpacks the meaning of God's saving work: Redeemed humans are transformed and made into agents of the operation of God's grace. Finally, Paul insists that God did for us what we could not do for ourselves.

In its logical progression Paul's argument runs this way: False perception of Christ > dramatic change > God gives this change > God's action is pure grace > Christians are now agents of God's grace > only God can work such change! Preachers will do well to follow Paul's lead.

Significance. Paul says that he once knew Christ according to the flesh. Then, Paul opposed him in ignorance, but according to Paul such is the response of this world to Jesus Christ. Indeed, Jesus Christ is not the savior this world would fabricate. In a world that keeps peace through strength and wins by intimidation, the crucified Christ doesn't cut a very impressive figure.

But Paul declares, "Things have changed—things can change!" Paul himself had a new point of view, and in his enthusiasm he sounds like a poet:

> Though we once knew Christ according to the flesh
> now we know him thus no longer
> so that
> if anyone is in Christ
> that person—man, woman, boy, or girl—is a new creation.
> The old things passed away—look, new things have come.
>
> (Author's paraphrase)

Paul writes about radical change. And for thousands and millions of Christians change happens as this world's standards come under the judgment of Jesus Christ. As people no longer living according to this world's standards—in Christ they are new creation!

We cannot help wondering, however, how this change takes place. Is it by mystery or magic, or is it a matter of luck or fate? Or is there someone who engineers the advent of the new creation? We wonder—and Paul has an answer, "All this is from God!" Those five words, "All this is from God!"—are the heart of the gospel. The good news about the new creation, about real change, about the radical transformation of broken sinful human life in a broken sinful world—change into a fresh redeemed existence—is that "All this is from God!"

And how do we know it? Because God was in Christ! In Christ God was and is reconciling the world. In Christ God steps forth into this world, into our lives, and we see him and he tells us what he's come for—to redeem us. God has come in Christ to do for us what we cannot—even with all the self-helps in the world—do for ourselves. God has come to forgive us. God has come to make us new.

But what does it mean to be reconciled? Paul insists that God reconciles us for ministry. To us has been entrusted the message of the gospel, the good news of God's reconciliation—that God in Christ was reconciling the world to himself. Christians are ambassadors for Christ. God has reconciled us—God has called us, God has elected us—in order to make his appeal through us to the rest of the world: Be reconciled to God!

The Gospel: *Luke 15:1-3, 11 b-32*

The Story of God's Grace and How We May Relate to It

Setting. As we continue to examine the portions of Luke's account of Jesus' journey to Jerusalem (9:51–19:27) we come to the fifteenth chapter of the Gospel, a recognizable unit of the story that presents a pair of paired-parables. Verses 1-3 provide the narrative setting in the ministry of Jesus, and vv. 4-10 relate the parables of "the lost sheep" (vv. 4-7) and "the lost coin" (vv. 8-10)—two parables better called "the diligent shepherd" and "the diligent sweeper." Next, vv. 11-32 recount the story of the prodigal son, a story with two distinct parts, vv. 11-24 and 25-32, united in fact by their true focus, "the loving father."

Structure. The setting of the lesson reveals the structure of the material. Verses 1-3 identify the different groups and reactions to the ministry of Jesus. Then, by moving to vv. 11-32 we find that in relation to "those who hear" and "those who complain" Luke recalls Jesus' parable of the father and his two sons. Although the parable is not allegory, the father with his openness, forgiveness, joy, generosity, and steadfastness is a symbol for God; whereas the sons are symbols of the ways humans (here, Jesus' audience) relate and react to God. Any congregation has some aspects of both sons in it, and most individuals have some of both sons in themselves. The sermon will follow the lead of the parable by telling of God and the manners in which we relate to God by pondering and drawing analogies to the characters and events in the story.

Significance. The story presents Jesus speaking in relation to two distinct groups in the course of his ministry. First, there are those who are marginalized in society and even shunned by self-satisfied and smug, rigidly religious people. These "sinners and tax-collectors" are able to hear the good news Jesus brings because they are outside the status quo and have little or nothing to lose. On the other hand, the account refers to Pharisees and scribes—that is, those who were quite concerned with proper religion and behavior. As we meet the second group here they are cast as incapable of hearing Jesus' radical message of God's acceptance of sinners—seemingly because they are overly secure in their own belief and practice. This presentation is something of a caricature, presenting the worst segment of a group as if it were the whole. For proclamation today we should recognize that there are self-contented pietists in the Church, but they do not make up the whole; yet, the preacher may follow Luke's lead and address the entire congregation as if they were cut of the same rotten strip of cloth—that is, working primarily against smugness rather than sinfulness (although religious smugness may be the worst kind of sin!).

Neither son in this story originally has a real relationship with the father. The younger son views the father as a source from which he can derive sufficient funds to live it up as he pleases. He takes his father's goodness for granted, abuses it, and only in his later sense of sorrow and loss is able to perceive the true character of the one of whose goodness he took advantage. The elder son can relate to his father only in a sense of being duty-bound, he is more a slave than a son; and so, he never really experiences the love and generosity of his father. The original ways in which we find the two sons relating to their father often are the ways in which we relate to God. The parable tells us that in these patterns we have no sense of who God is, and we do not have a valid relationship.

But the parable also calls us away from where we are to where God wills for us to be. In the same way that the younger son "came to himself" as he pondered the reality of the person of his father, we can hear this story from Jesus and realize that God's goodness means we are forgiven and invited to celebrate with God the establishment of a new, loving relationship. Moreover, as we stand with the older son, overly secure in the knowledge of our faithfulness in service to God, we may see that we are outside the experience of God's grace; but, now, God calls us into the joyful establishment of a new sense of God's goodness. We may stand apart from God either in sin or in a sense of religious superiority. In either case, the parable calls us to recognize the separation and to see that God wills a new relationship characterized by joy rather than greed or mere duty.

In a final word for preaching let us step back from the story to form a strategy for proclamation. Today, unfortunately, some members of a congregation may be unable to hear the gospel in this story because of the cast of male characters. That the parable is not about God's maleness should be evident from the preceding parable of the sweeper in which the ever-pursuing love of God is cast as a female character. Some care may be necessary in crafting a sermon, so that God's all-encompassing love, forgiveness, and call may be heard by all and not hindered by a contemporary sensibility. Approaching this issue directly, however, runs the risk in some contexts of derailing the sermon, so that a well-conceived and executed indirect handling of the matter may prove the best solution.

Lent 4: The Celebration

Today has been known in the Western Church as *Laetare,* or Rejoice, Sunday, because the first word in the Latin introit is "Laetare." It signaled a brief respite from the Lenten rigors, and the churches in Rome changed from purple to rose colored vestments (the origin of rose-colored candles on the Third Sunday of Advent in order to make the Advent observance parallel that of Lent). The actual text of the introit calls upon Jerusalem to rejoice, and it was chosen to complement the epistle in the previous one-year cycle, which was Galatians 4:22-31, and which says "that Jerusalem which is above is free, which is our mother." That the introit has been retained even though it has reference to none of the new sets of lessons gives it a rather vestigial character. Collectors of liturgical trivia might be interested to know, however, that the tune Materna ("O beautiful for spacious skies") was composed, and so derived its name, for a hymn written for this day, "O mother dear, Jerusalem." In England the day is still popularly known as Mothering Sunday or Refreshment Sunday (because the former Gospel reading was the feeding of the multitude), and it has something of a homecoming aspect to it.

Mothering Sunday might still not be an inappropriate designation for today since the lessons we encounter in both the Old Testament and Gospel readings are concerned about people who go home and who find refreshment. The sharing of the Passover in the promised land and the feast prepared for the returned prodigal evoke images of the heavenly banquet which we anticipate by faith at every Eucharist. This makes Psalm 34:8 a good choice for today's introit or call to worship.

Even though the Gospel reading may seem to be long, the introductory verses (1-3) should not be omitted. They are important in order to provide the context and background for the parable. The following Wesley stanza, sung to a long meter tune, might be used either before or immediately after the reading of the Gospel.

> O thou whom once they flocked to hear,
> thy words to hear, thy power to feel;
> suffer the sinners to draw near,
> and graciously receive us still.

The references to the new creation in the epistle reading suggest the use of "Love Divine, All Loves Excelling" with its line, "finish, then, thy new creation."

Fifth Sunday in Lent

Old Testament Texts

Isaiah 43:16-21 is an oracle of salvation that recalls the crossing of the water and the wandering in the desert. Psalm 126 is a poem about Israel's reversal of fortune.

The Lesson: *Isaiah 43:16-21*

An Oracle of Salvation

Setting. Isaiah 43:16-21 is an oracle of salvation. The expected structure of an oracle of salvation, includes (1) a community lament, (2) a proclamation of salvation, and (3) a glimpse of the end result of God's salvation. Isaiah 43:16-21 has departed from this form by not including a community lament. Instead, a recounting of the Exodus has taken its place.

Structure. The text can be outlined in the following way: (1) divine recounting of the Exodus (vv. 16-17), (2) the proclamation of a new salvation (vv. 18-19), and (3) the end result of this new salvation: water in the wilderness, honor to God by creatures, and praise of God by the people of God (vv. 20-21).

Significance. The central point of the salvation oracle in 43:16-21 is the emphasis on discontinuity between the former things and a new thing that God is about to do. If this becomes the focus for preaching, care must be given to interpret this text in the larger context of Second Isaiah. If read in isolation the salvation oracle looks as though it is a denial of past tradition, because the prophet proclaims, "Do not remember the former things." And, instead, he turns the attention of his audience to a "new thing" that is about "to spring forth." Second Isaiah is a prophet steeped in tradition, who frequently calls Israel to affirm in the present time the power of God that was evident in past events. The contrast between the former things and new thing in 43:16-21 should be interpreted in this vein. Exilic Israel had come to believe that the best was behind them, with the result that past tradition came to embody a lost golden age. The oracle of salvation does not deny the significance of the past Exodus. In fact it is almost as if the description of the Exodus in vv. 16-17 has become part of the divine name (an epithet). Note the syntax of these verses: "Thus says the LORD, who . . . , who. . . ." The two subordinate clauses that begin with "who" provide content to the name by describing the past action of God. But God is not content with past laurels. The prophet is concerned that exilic Israel not be burdened by the framework of the past, but use it to see a new picture of God's salvation in the present. There certainly is discontinuity in this proclamation. Unforeseen things are about to happen, but these saving events will be an extension of past Exodus tradition and not a departure from it.

The Response: *Psalm 126*

A Reversal of Fortune

Setting. Psalm 126 is about a reversal of fortune. Two reversals are described in vv. 1-3 and in v. 4. Verses 1-3 refer to the reversal of fortune for Zion, while v. 4 focuses on the worshiping community. Ambiguity concerning the temporal relationship between these two points of focus yields two different interpretations of the psalm.

Structure. Psalm 126 can be separated into two or three parts. Verses 1-3 focus on Zion, v. 4 is a petition by the community, and vv. 5-6 present words of promise or confidence.

Significance. Scholars debate whether the restoration of Zion in vv. 1-3 should be read as a future or as a past event. Thus, is the psalm eschatological in its orientation or a reflection on history? If the psalm is read as a future hope, then the petition in v. 4 is a plea for the realization of vv. 1-3, and vv. 5-6 function as prophetic promise. If the psalm is read as a reflection on a past event, then v. 4 is a more specific plea that the people be restored along with Zion, or it is a petition of renewal, to which vv. 5-6 become a statement of confidence. This ambiguity invites the preacher or worship leader to determine the appropriate reading of the psalm for each specific community. When the psalm is read as a response to the oracle of salvation in Isaiah 43:16-21 it serves as a continuation of promised salvation that is sketched out by the prophet.

New Testament Texts

The reading from Philippians urges believers forward in faith and away from the lure of self-righteous contentment, a theme that has been sounded repeatedly in this Lenten season. The story of Jesus' anointing with "nard" anticipates the anointing of Jesus' crucified body and reminds us that the call to examine ourselves in relation to God is founded upon the saving work of God in the costly death of Jesus. Thus, we are situated but not stuck in Lent, and as we approach the end of the forty days, we prepare to remember Good Friday and even Easter.

The Epistle: *Philippians 3:4b-14*

Called from Contentment to Suffering and Glory

Setting. In the opening portion of Philippians, 1:12-26, Paul discussed his situation (he was in jail), and then he issued a series of exhortations, 1:27–2:18. In a similar way, in 2:19–3:1, Paul discusses his plans for the future, and then he issues further directions (warnings and admonitions) in 3:2-21. The verses for this Sunday's epistle reading come in this second section of pointed prescriptions. Unfortunately the lectionary begins the lesson with 3:4*b*. This takes the larger coherent statement in 3:4*b*-14 out of context. The result, upon hearing the reading, may be disastrous. In 3:2-4*a* Paul warns the Philippians to be on guard against those who advocate Jewish observances (perhaps the law). Against the claims to authority of those who would advocate Jewish practices in the context of the church, Paul delineates his own credentials. Thus, in 3:4*b*-14 Paul is arguing against opponents, not simply presenting his accomplishments. If vv. 4*b*-14 are read in isolation from vv. 2-4*a* one runs the danger of perpetuating the serious, distorting misperception of Paul as an arrogant, boastful egomaniac. Moreover, stopping the lesson after v. 14 rather than v. 16 leaves Paul's statements at the level of himself and never applies them to the life of the congregation as Paul does in 3:15-16. Unless we are called to preach Paul, we should expand the text. Therefore, the commentary that follows deals with 3:2-16.

Structure. In 3:2-4*a* Paul turns his remarks to the Philippians in a new, even surprising direction—he warns against falling prey to those advocating Jewish practices. In order to show that he understands well the advice he is giving, in vv. 4*b*-6 Paul recites his own Jewish credentials. Then, in vv. 7-11 he explains why he himself turned away from such patterns of piety. Next, in vv. 12-14, Paul qualifies his remarks by telling how his life as a Christian is a dynamic, ongoing challenge. Finally, in vv. 15-16, Paul makes an appeal to the Philippians, which he bases on the foregoing statements.

Significance. This is a striking passage, which if read carefully can overturn some of our most precious and tenaciously held misunderstandings about early Christian life and faith. First, we should see clearly that not all early Christians agreed on what it meant to be a faithful follower of Christ and how, in turn, believers were to live. Even the very earliest Christians had to struggle with the real issues of belief and practice that confront us today. Thus, we find in scripture not only the parameters for our lives as disciples, but also testimony to the necessity of our struggle to work out our salvation with faithful fear and trembling.

Paul and some other professing believers had sharp differences of opinions. Apparently Paul's opponents attempted to win the day by claiming an authority based upon their Jewish credentials. In response, Paul recites his own qualifications. Many misleading sermons, frequently well off the interpretive mark, have been preached on vv. 4-11. Indeed, we should recognize that Paul is neither guilty nor disillusioned as he looks back on his life in Judaism; rather, he was quite content and can refer to his former accomplishments as "gain." But now he is changed, and the gain is "loss" (one does not refer to getting rid of a bad thing as a loss). Why? Because of Christ. Paul speaks here from the retrospective outlook of Christian faith.

He moves from solution to plight, not from dilemma to remedy. In Christ, by Christ, and because of Christ Paul's whole outlook and value-system was radically altered. Now Paul understands that righteousness is God's work, and it comes to humans as a gift of grace sustained by Christ; righteousness is not a humanly maintained status in relation to God. No, God does the doing of righteousness, and humans have it from start to finish as grace. This may prove hard to swallow. Perhaps that is why Paul's opponents are advocating Jewish practices. They cannot believe that they do not somehow need to throw their human weight in with the work of God in Christ for their salvation.

In turn, Paul speaks from his new Christian perspective, talking of the hope instilled by his faith. By virtue of being in Christ and knowing him, Paul is able not only to tolerate suffering, but because he suffers for Christ, he finds his suffering meaningful. Moreover, in Christ he looks beyond the present to the future glory he anticipates because of the resurrection of Christ. And, lest he be misunderstood, Paul declares that he has not yet obtained the glory of the resurrection in this life. That glory is for the future; so that in the present, in faith, Paul presses on. If we hear the apostle well, we understand that the call to Christ is not an order to be "at ease"; rather, we are called to move on, perhaps in "double time." Paul seems assured of the Philippians' capacity to hear, because he believes that whatever understanding they enjoy comes to them from the work of God among them; and God's work ultimately unites believers, despite the real differences, which Paul recognizes and which motivated his words in this passage.

The Gospel: *John 12:1-8*

The Focus and Nature of Christian Gratitude

Setting. We must note where this story comes in the Fourth Gospel. Interpreters speak of two major portions of John: John 1–12 is called "the book of signs," because it contains an account of selected and revealing deeds of Jesus that manifested his glory and indicated to those of faith who he was; then, John 13–21 is called "the book of glory," for in these chapters we read of the last days of

Jesus' life, Passion, death, resurrection, and his gift of the Holy Spirit—together, the substance of Jesus' "glorification."

Our lesson comes toward the end of the signs-section and signals a transition as it anticipates the burial of Jesus—and so, his Passion (perhaps also the Resurrection and the gift of the Spirit). Moreover, that Jesus came in Bethany to an atmosphere of hostility is clear from the immediately preceding portion of the Gospel—see 11:45-57, especially 11:53, 57. The story is itself a kind of "sign" about Jesus' work.

Structure. The narrative situates Jesus in Bethany at a banquet in the company of Lazarus, Martha, and Mary. We learn of Mary's anointing Jesus' feet with costly ointment. In turn, Judas objects. This development gives the author of John an opportunity to comment on Judas' hypocritical dishonesty. As always in John, however, Jesus has the final word. The complex statement is confrontational, prophetic, and revelatory. Jesus' words both conclude and dominate the account. Thus, the focus is taken off both Mary's extravagance and Judas' malodorous character.

Significance. Anyone preparing to preach on this lesson should compare Matthew 26:6-13; Mark 14:3-9; and Luke 7:36-50. Read in conjunction with the other accounts of the anointing of Jesus, this story raises far more questions than anyone can answer. For example, When was Jesus anointed? Where did this take place? Was he anointed on the head or the feet? Who did the anointing? How did she do it? Who objected? Why? What did Jesus say? There are more questions, and no one has full or sufficient answers. Thus, in traditional piety people usually know a homogenized version of this story; and, perhaps most tragically, they twist the harmonized account to whatever end they wish. Thus, one former President of the United States loosely quoted Jesus' words about the poor, to defend cutting relief programs to those in poverty.

The only real remedy to the impossible interpretive situation and the steady abuse of the account(s) of this event is to take the story as directly as possible in the terms that each particular evangelist presents it. Thus, we must let John be John, not ask him to be Mark or Luke—and so also with Mark and Luke. If we approach John's account in this manner, we must take seriously the mood of the narrative, the development of the story, and move with the text to where it takes us!

The story begins by placing Jesus in an atmosphere that recalls and celebrates his many wondrous deeds. The sermon should point to and celebrate the life and work of Jesus with its telling manifestations of the power and will of God. In turn, the story focuses on the responses of humans to Jesus' ministry. What Jesus did produced gratitude and joy, even celebration. The sermon may recall how the gospel affects persons today so that they are moved in sheer gratitude to celebrate the goodness of God's work in Jesus Christ. Yet, lest the mood of festivity run wild, the story brings in the sour, self-centered resentment of one who was less than enthused about Jesus' ministry and the joyous reaction of others to it. Simply omitting this part of the story, however, may impart a saccharin sweetness to the rest of the account and, thus, to the preaching! The next portion of the story, which moves to refer to the death of Jesus, makes little sense without some recognition of real hostility that he encountered in his life and work. A frank recognition that the whole world is not singing Jesus' praises may take a variety of forms.

Jesus' declaration exposes the hypocrisy of Judas' objection and points to the cross and resurrection—that is, to Jesus' costly glory achieved in the context of God's saving work in relation to humankind. The difficult reference to the poor surely means that if we are truly grateful to God for the joy of salvation we know in Christ, then, now that our Lord has died and been raised, we have—in relation to the poor—a clear opportunity to express our gratitude. Perhaps we will even act as Mary did—that is, with extravagance. Thus, the story ends with a christologically focused call to take seriously the real needs of others!

Lent 5: The Celebration

The water imagery of the Old Testament reading and the psalm and the theme of anointing in the Gospel reading is intended to lead us into a deeper meditation upon the meaning of the baptisms that will be celebrated at Easter and of our own baptisms as well. The epistle reading provides a context in which to think about living out our baptisms, particularly if the lesson is expanded, as recommended in the above commentary, to Philippians 3:2-16.

Philippians 3:10-11 is a description of what it means to be baptized: "to know Christ and the power of his resurrection and the sharing of his sufferings by becoming like him in his death, if somehow I may attain the resurrection from the dead." It is this which is symbolized by Christian baptism when we go under the water as a sign of death and come out again as a sign of the resurrection. What is striking about this passage is that for Paul this new life in Christ is a dynamic, not a static, event. Even though he has been baptized into the death and resurrection of Christ, he knows that he has not already reached the final eschatological realization of it ("Not that I have already obtained this or have already reached the goal"), but the remainder of his life is to be a living out of the meaning of his baptism. His baptism is an ongoing experience of salvation. This can be a significant pastoral word to those who agonize about rebaptism and who think that baptism is somehow supposed to be the last word in the experience of salvation. For Paul the word of baptism comes nearer to the beginning of the sentence. It is closer to the truth to say "I am baptized" than "I was baptized," as though baptism is ever a completed act.

The Gospel reading calls to mind that in many churches the practice of anointing with chrism is again accompanying the rite of baptism. Mary anoints Jesus as testimony that he is the Messiah, the anointed one. We are anointed in baptism as a sign that he has made us kings and priests, because anointing in biblical times was part of their induction into office.

Congregations that use sung antiphons or responses to the psalm might today wish to use the line, "We shall come rejoicing, bringing in the sheaves," from the old gospel hymn. Other music in the service, however, should now begin to focus more upon the coming observance of the Passion. A particularly fitting hymn to connect epistle and Gospel is "Jesus, the Very Thought of Thee" (*AMEC Bicentennial Hymnal*, no. 464; *Hymnal: A Worship Book*, no. 588; *The Hymnal of the United Church of Christ*, no. 267; *The Hymnal 1982*, no. 642; *Hymns for the Family of God*, no. 465; *Worship the Lord: Hymnal of the Church of God*, no. 466).

"THE GREAT REDEEMING WORK": PRAISE, PRAYER, AND PREACHING IN HOLY WEEK

This week, culminating in the celebration of the resurrection, is at the heart of the Church's liturgical life, for it gives meaning to all the Church does the rest of the year. It is therefore important that the ordering of public worship and the preparation of sermons be done with a concern for "the basics," for retelling and remembering the story of salvation in such a dynamic fashion that the participants may become aware of their own involvement in God's story.

The posture of the worshiping Church is not that of those who are ignorant of how the story is going to turn out, or of the original disciples as they experienced the horror of the crucifixion and the fear of a similar fate. We do not enter Holy Week ignorant of Easter Day, and that fact informs the character of our celebration. As a recent hymn puts it:

> They could not know, as we do now,
> how glorious is that crown;
> that thorns would flower upon your brow,
> your sorrows heal our own.
> *(The United Methodist Hymnal,* no. 285)

Celebration is still an appropriate word, even for the Good Friday liturgy, because the Church's celebration is always of God's triumph over sin and death, as a sixth-century hymnwriter knew:

> Sing, my tongue, the glorious battle,
> sing the ending of the fray;
> now above the cross, the trophy,
> sound the loud triumphant lay;
> tell how Christ, the world's Redeemer,
> as a victim won the day.
> *(The United Methodist Hymnal,* no. 296)

Holy Week may be divided into three sections: (1) the Sunday of the Passion, or Palm Sunday; (2) Monday, Tuesday, and Wednesday; and (3) the Paschal Triduum [three days] of Maundy Thursday, Good Friday, and Easter Day—which, in its turn, may have the vigil or night service and the service during the day. Because of space limitations, this year's volume will deal only with the lessons of Passion Sunday and Maundy or Holy Thursday. Good Friday's lessons will be found in the Year B volume, the Easter Vigil's in Year A, Easter Day's in Year B.

Perhaps the greatest surprise for many in the new structuring of the lectionary and calendar is the changed approach to Palm Sunday, which is now referred to as The Sunday of the Passion or as Passion/Palm Sunday, but not as Palm Sunday only. This means, of course, that the Fifth Sunday in Lent is no longer called Passion Sunday, as it was in the old calendar. It remains simply the Fifth Sunday in Lent. This is to emphasize the centrality of the Passion of Christ in the liturgical celebrations of Holy Week itself, and to prepare ourselves more fully for the solemn observance of the Triduum. Palm Sunday, then, is neither a kind of dry-run for Easter, nor is it intended to lay all the emphasis upon the triumphal entry in such a way as to allow those who only attend church on Sunday to miss the message of the cross. It is at least Passion/Palm Sunday, reminding us of the reason for the entry into Jerusalem.

Holy Week, by its very character as the time for specific remembering of the events of the Passion, stands out from the rest of Lent. This is accented visually by changing from the purple paraments or the Lenten array to a somber blood-red color for paraments and vestments. Ideally these should be designed for this week in particular, rather than using the same red set as will appear at Pentecost. The red itself should be different in hue, darker than the brighter, red-orange of Pentecost.

The service for Passion/Palm Sunday is divided into two parts. The first is the Entrance Rite (the Liturgy of the Palms), which centers around the narrative of the entry into Jerusalem. This may begin out-of-doors or in the parish hall and then include a procession of all the people into the church for the second major part (the Liturgy of the Passion), which centers around the reading of the Passion narrative from whichever is the controlling Gospel for the year. (The Passion according to St. John is always read on Good Friday.) There should be some obvious contrast between the "Hosannas" of the first part and the "Crucify!" of the second. The entry into the church should begin to mark a difference in emphasis as the people prepare to hear the Old Testament lesson. By the conclusion of the service the congregation should be thinking seriously of what it means to spend the ensuing week in the shadow of the cross.

In the event of inclement weather or for some other reason the entire service needs to be done within the church itself, proper planning can still provide for a processional. The choir and minister should enter the chancel in silence and as unobtrusively as possible. When all are in place, then the minister greets the people and offers an appropriate opening prayer. In Year C Luke 19:28-40 is read and then there may be a blessing and distribution of the branches (if they have not been distributed at the door upon arrival). Notice that these should be branches that are waveable. Then, during the singing of such hymns as "All Glory, Laud, and Honor" and "Hosanna, Loud Hosanna," the choir leaves the chancel, processes through and around the nave, returning back up the center aisle into the chancel. It is appropriate that the people file out of the pews and process around with the choir. This is liturgical dance at its most basic and most inclusive, since one does not need any sense of rhythm to participate!

Great care needs to be taken in preparing for any dramatic reading of the Passion narrative. Participants should be well-rehearsed. Scripts are available that divide the lesson up into readers' parts. The preparation for this reading may well involve a special Lenten study group as the readers explore the Passion narrative in intensive Bible study. This may be a project for the confirmation class, particularly if its participation and leadership can compensate for having the actual confirmations on this day rather than waiting until the more temporally significant Eastertide.

The lessons for Monday, Tuesday, and Wednesday in Holy Week are the same all three years of the lectionary cycle. Their intent is not to review the events of the original Holy Week day by day, but to provide the faithful with a context within which to prepare to participate fully in the celebration of the mysteries of our salvation during the Triduum. The Old Testament lessons (Mon., Isaiah 42:1-9; Tue., Isaiah 49:1-7; Wed., Isaiah 50:4-9*a*) are from the first three servant songs and remind us of the servant character of the Messiah. The epistle lessons (Mon., Hebrews 9:11-15; Tue., I Corinthians 1:18-31; Wed., Hebrews 12:1-3) direct our thoughts to the themes of the cross and atonement. The Gospel readings (Mon., John 12:1-11; Tue., John 12:20-36; Wed., John 13:21-32) serve respectively to identify Jesus as God's anointed, whose death is part of a divine necessity, resulting in the glorification of both God and Christ.

Maundy Thursday is referred to in the Revised Common Lectionary as "Holy Thursday," presumably following the new Roman Catholic usage. A strong case may be made for "Maundy," however, based on the concluding verse of the Gospel (John 13:1-17, 34): "a new commandment I give to you." "Maundy" derives from *mandatum,* the Latin word for "commandment." It is this new commandment that Jesus illustrates at the Last Supper by washing the disciples' feet, which local congregations may observe on this day by the liturgical washing of one another's feet. For congregations that are hesitant to consider the washing of feet, Heather Murray Elkins has devised a "Liturgy of Basins," which is published by the Order of St. Luke in *Sacramental Life* (July/August 1989). The service is based on Jewish hand washing and "offers the means for both corporate and private admission of sin, and assurance of pardon."

The primary emphases of the day are the remembrance of the holy meal that Jesus celebrated with the disciples "on the night in which he was given up for us" (the Last Supper) and thanksgiving for the institution of that holy meal of remembrance through which he has been present with the Church through the ages (the Lord's Supper). The new Roman Catholic practice has been to emphasize the former since they have the feast of Corpus Christi on which to do the latter. Protestant churches, particularly those that celebrate the Lord's Supper only occasionally, can balance these emphases. White paraments rather than passion-red might be more appropriate for this service. Care should be taken not to give the impression of playacting the Last Supper and thus identifying that meal as the only one which informs the meaning of the Lord's Supper. Even on Maundy Thursday this is still the bridal feast of the Lamb and is celebrated by a Church that has had the Emmaus experience. It is purposeful that the lessons for this service do not include any of the synoptic accounts of the Last Supper. What we hear about the Last Supper is from Paul who identifies all later commemorations as eschatological proclamation. The Gospel lesson is from John, who does not describe the actual meal at all. Rather, his emphasis is on the washing of the disciples' feet, with Jesus doing a kind of "show and tell" about the meaning of his ministry.

Planners of worship for Maundy Thursday might keep in mind the balance between the historical event two thousand years ago and its identification with the Passover experience of Israel, and the present event in which Christ still makes himself available to his people and makes them a sacrament for the world. If the Washing of Feet is observed, it is natural to have it follow the reading of the Gospel and the sermon. Following that, the offertory hymn or anthem should be one of praise and thanksgiving for the gift of Holy Communion. Hymns during Communion should also express joy for the sacrament, rather than being Good Friday/crucifixion fare. It is after Communion that the aspect of the service changes and the people prepare to recall the suffering and death of Jesus.

Following the Prayer after Communion, a versicle and response might be used:

V. And when they had sung a hymn:

R: They went out to the Mount of Olives.

Then, while the congregation sings a hymn such as " 'Tis Midnight, and on Olive's Brow," the altar and chancel are stripped of all decoration. The altar cross is veiled in dark red or black, and the people leave in silence.

The Good Friday service should be thought of as a continuation of the Maundy Thursday service. The people return in silence to the setting that they left the night before. The service begins in silence and proceeds quickly to the lessons and the reading of St. John's Passion. This reading may also be done with members of the congregation taking the various parts, the congregation as a whole being the crowd. The sermon today is expected to deal with any of the major themes that emerge from the lessons. The preacher's first task will be to limit carefully how much one sermon can deal with! Additional liturgical resources can be found in *The Book of Common Prayer* and the *New Handbook of the Christian Year*.

Passion Sunday

Old Testament Texts

The Old Testament lessons are very appropriate for Passion Sunday. Isaiah 50:4-9a explores the call of the suffering servant, while Psalm 31:9-16 is a lament from the perspective of one who is suffering. As we will see both of these lessons share a similar three-part structure and probe the meaning of suffering from slightly different perspectives.

The Lesson: *Isaiah 50:4-9a*

A Call to Discipleship

Setting. Isaiah 50:4-9a is the third of the suffering servant songs (Isaiah 42:1-4[5-9]; 49:1-6; 50:4-9a; 52:13–53:12). The first song was the lesson for Epiphany in Year A. You may want to refer to this lesson for a discussion of the individual and collective interpretations of these songs, since that discussion also applies to our present lesson. In the first servant song (Isaiah 42:1-4[5-9]) God is the primary speaker in declaring the choice of the servant. In the second song (Isaiah 49:1-6) the servant affirms his call already from the womb, but then doubts the purpose of it all with the claim that he has labored in vain. This song ends with the divine proclamation that the servant has not labored in vain, but is called to be a light to the nations. The lesson for this Passion Sunday is an individual lament (or an individual psalm of confidence) by the suffering servant. Here there is no longer any doubt about the purposefulness of his call. The servant knows that he is called to be God's pupil or disciple no matter what circumstances befall him.

Structure. Isaiah 50:4-9*a* separates into three parts. In vv. 4-5*aa* the servant proclaims his call. This opening section is framed by the phrase, "The Lord GOD has given me the tongue . . . has opened my ear. . . ." Verses 5*ab*-6 describe the servants training in discipleship. The song closes in vv. 7-9*a* with the suffering servant confessing the reliability of God's salvation. This closing unit is framed with the confession, "For the Lord GOD helps me. . . ."

Significance. The third suffering servant song presents a blueprint for discipleship, for it illustrates how theory and praxis must be one for any follower of GOD. The opening section of the song in vv. 4-5*aa* roots the authority of the servant in the call of God. In the opening and closing phrase, "The Lord GOD has . . . ," the servant makes it clear that he has been called to speak for God (the Lord has given him a tongue) and to hear the word of God (the Lord has opened his ear). The servant then tells us that his commissioning to hear God's word is for the purpose of discipleship. We are told in v. 4 that every morning God awakens the servant so that he is able to hear God's instruction like a pupil (Hebrew, *limmudim*; NRSV translation, "to listen as those who are taught"). The second section of the song is marked in v. 5*ab*, when the servant refers to himself and his present situation. In vv. 5*ab*-6 the servant outlines his training in discipleship. Here the work of God is translated into action. The servant does not rebel from God's instruction, but accepts suffering in the present time. The final section (vv. 7-9*a*) shifts the focus back to God and in so doing the servant provides the content of what he has learned as God's disciple, which now allows him to endure suffering. The content of God's tutoring is the proclamation of salvation that frames this unit in vv. 7 and 9 ("The Lord GOD helps me"). This confession allows for further affirmations about God's salvation by the servant in v. 7 and a direct address to his oppressors in v. 8. In v. 7 the two "therefores" state the servant's resolve to be a disciple, because God is near. In vv. 8-9*a* the servant addresses his opponents through a series of questions: Who will contend with me? Who is my adversary? Who will declare me guilty? The answer, of course, is no one.

The striking thing about this suffering servant song, which must be emphasized in preaching, is how easily it moves between the images of student and suffering activist, between knowing the content of salvation in the classroom and doing the work of salvation. Neither theory nor praxis is allowed a special role over the other in the servant's soliloquy on discipleship. The servant is able to endure suffering because he knows that God is savior. Here doing is knowing and knowing is doing. This inseparable symbiosis goes to the heart of Passion Sunday.

The Response: *Psalm 31:9-16*

Living on God's Time

Setting. Psalm 31:9-16 builds on Isaiah 50:4-9*a*. It, too, is a psalm about suffering. It builds on Isaiah 50:4-9*a* because Psalm 31:9-16 explores the interior dimensions of the psalmist during the time of suffering in a way that the suffering servant song did not. Although the suffering of the servant in Isaiah 50:4-9*a* was intense, the point of view of the passage was on God and God's reliability during times of suffering. Because of this focus we were never allowed to separate the servant's suffering from God's presence and salvation. Because of this Isaiah 50:4-9*a* is probably best categorized as a song of confidence. Psalm 31:6-16 takes us further away from the security of God's salvation by exploring the experience of suffering itself. By taking us inside the experience of the suffering psalmist (especially in vv. 11-13) Psalm 31:9-16 becomes a true lament, where confessing the salvation of God is not enough. God must be called upon directly for salvation.

Structure. The psalm for this Sunday is only a fraction of Psalm 31. Most scholars would divide the psalm between vv. 1-8 and 9-24. There is debate, however, on how these two parts are meant to interrelate. Each section appears to be an independent lament. Are they separate psalms that have been brought together? Are they parallel psalms that describe the same experience with increasing intensity? In addition to these larger questions of structure, we should note that a more natural break in the psalm would have been vv. 9-18, since vv. 19-24 is a song of praise that concludes the previous laments (vv. 1-8, 9-18). This discussion of the larger context of Psalm 31 suggests that vv. 9-16 can function well as a unit, even though the call for salvation actually extends through vv. 17-18. Psalm 31:9-16 can be separated into three parts: a call for salvation in vv. 9-10, a description of the psalmist's situation in vv. 11-13, and a confession in, along with a renewed call for, God's salvation in vv. 15-16.

Significance. The structure of Psalm 31:9-16 provides an interesting parallel to the suffering servant song of Isaiah 50:4-9*a*, because it separates into three parts that show roughly the same movement: from a focus on God, to the experience of the psalmist/suffering servant, and then back to God. As noted above, however, the movement of Psalm 31:9-16 takes us much more deeply into the experience of the psalmist, which makes this more of a lament than a song of confidence. Although God is the object of the psalm, and, indeed, looms large beneath the surface in every verse, it is the experience of the psalmist, who is presently at a great distance from God's salvation, that takes up most of the imagery. The opening call for salvation in vv. 9-10 ("Be gracious to me, O LORD") gives way immediately to a physical description of the psalmist. Not only are his eyes dissolving (Hebrew, '*ss*; NRSV, wastes) from grief, but his very bones are also dissolving. Verses 11-13 move us from a physical to a social description of the psalmist. Here we learn that this person radiates dread (Hebrew, *herpa*; NRSV, the scorn of) to both friends and enemies (v. 11). She is the walking dead (v. 12). This is not idealized suffering. In fact there is no confidence here at all—nothing to grab on to because terror is on every side (v. 13). Up to this point Psalm 31 has described the agony of social alienation and physical breakdown from personal threat. Yet it is here that life itself is also clearly seen for what it is: We all live on God's time (v. 15). This revelation brings the psalmist outside of herself and back to God with a confession of trust along with a renewed call for salvation in vv. 14-16. In reading this psalm and in identifying with the psalmist, we move through the dark pit and dread of Passion Sunday.

New Testament Texts

Both texts are concerned with the Passion and death of Jesus. The brief liturgical piece in Philippians 2 speaks of the "mind" of Christ, indicating the selfless, sacrificial obedience which brought Christ to his death on the cross. The long lesson from Luke takes us through a selected portion of Luke's Passion narrative from the time that Jesus sat at the Last Supper with the apostles until the notice about resting on the Sabbath that comes immediately after the report of the burial of Jesus. The epistle reading invites vivid preaching whereas the very length of the Gospel lesson suggests dramatic reading of the text, perhaps woven together with exposition following the various paragraphs of the material or with a pointed summary of major themes and concerns at the conclusion of the whole.

The Epistle: *Philippians 2:5-11*

Having the Mind of Christ

Setting. The Philippian congregation was the first European church founded by Paul, and it was one with which he maintained a very positive relationship. He was in prison at the time he penned this letter; and he seems to have written for several reasons: (1) to thank the Philippians for their support, physical and spiritual; (2) to discuss Epaphroditus's visit to him in behalf of the Philippians; and (3) to address difficulties and potential problems in the life of the church. Paul spends time early in the body of the letter exhorting the Philippians to unity, beginning at 1:27. In the course of that admonition he holds Christ himself up in a formal fashion as the model and source of Christian harmony.

Structure. Since the late 1920s innumerable scholars have studied Philippians 2:(5)6-11, attempting both to demonstrate that this portion of Philippians is a "Christ-hymn" from the life of the early church and to determine the hymn's structure, origin, authorship, and theology. At the heart of debate about structure is whether the "hymn" is concerned with celebrating two movements (Christ's humble emptying into human form and Christ's exaltation to heavenly Lordship) or three states (preexistence/human life/resurrection-exaltation). While these issues are still studied and debated, interpreters are moving toward a middle ground that recognizes the importance of all the elements of both schemes. Whatever the analysis, however, v. 5 is regarded as prose, leading up to the hymn; and vv. 6-11 are seen as the "hymn" per se.

Significance. It is crucial to recognize the range and force of the theological and christological statements contained in this text. Five major thoughts are articulated: First, the remarks about Jesus Christ in the form of God is a metaphorical expression of the conviction of his preexistence. With notable exceptions, few interpreters read the line otherwise. The importance of this interpretation should not be missed. Here, in one of the earliest preserved documents of Christianity is the confession of Christ's preexistence. Often historians assume that belief in preexistence came later in the development of Christian doctrine, but Philippians is testimony to the contrary. Equally remarkable is that Paul, the former Jew, includes and approves such a belief, for there is no evidence that Paul had abandoned Jewish monotheism to make this statement. Second, Christ's earthly existence is declared by using the metaphor of slavery. What does it mean to say that Christ took the form of a slave? The metaphor points to his humble obedience to the will of God and to his faithful service to his fellow human beings as he did God's will. Third, we hear of Christ's death. The mention of the cross in connection with the death points to the degree of humiliation Christ suffered in order to be faithful to God and humankind. His service was costly. He did not live to a ripe old age and enjoy the fruits of his happy life of service. Indirectly Paul is telling the Philippians (and us) that the Lord died in order to be obedient and faithful—thus, what can disciples expect? Fourth, Christ's exaltation-resurrection is declared. The phrase, "wherefore also God," introduces this element of the confession. Clearly Christ's being raised and his subsequent exalted status are God's work. Notice too that the language ("wherefore") reaches back and relates God's action to Christ's own emptying and self-sacrifice. Fifth, we learn of Christ's cosmic rule. His self-giving unto death, which issued in God's exalting him makes him the ruler of the cosmos. The phrases describing the "knees" indicates that all the denizens of heaven, earth, and hell will acknowledge Christ's rule. And the point of that rule is given with the words "unto the glory of God the Father."

The Gospel: *Luke 22:14–23:56*

"And He Was Reckoned with Transgressors"

Setting. By beginning the lesson at 22:14 the lectionary passes over the notice about Passover drawing near, the report of the Jewish leaders conspiring against Jesus, Satan's entering Judas, and the account of the preparation of the Passover meal at Jesus' direction. If the main substance of proclamation will be the dramatic reading of Luke's Passion narrative, then, one may well drop back and begin the reading from 22:1 to reclaim these important preliminary items that give particular sense to the narrative that follows.

Structure. One event leads to another. Unlike most of the material in the Gospel the recognizable sections of the Passion narrative are not capable of freestanding or independent existence; rather, the parts cohere to form a complex but coordinated whole. Thus, Luke takes us from the table to the tomb. The order of the events is similar to that found in Mark's Passion narrative, although there are noticeable shifts in the sequence of occurrences, and Luke offers material that goes beyond the content of Mark's account. Careful comparison of Luke and Mark (and Matthew) helps one perceive Luke's emphases and interests in presenting the story of Jesus' Passion, and directs us in interpreting the account.

Significance. As we move through Luke's presentation, a number of items demand our attention and merit commentary. The following selective remarks should point the way either for reading or preaching this lesson.

First, as Jesus speaks at the Last Supper his words interpret the bread and the second cup in relation to his forthcoming death. We learn that Jesus gives himself in our behalf, according to God's will, for our salvation. We should notice in Jesus' opening lines over the first cup that he did not partake of this Passover meal, despite his deep longing to do so. His words point to and even beyond the cross to the full-form coming of the Kingdom, so that we learn that the time that lies ahead has intense eschatological significance.

Second, Jesus' statements about the betrayer leads to a dispute among the disciples over greatness (compare Mark 10:41-45 and Matthew 20:24-28). In turn, Jesus speaks in the context of the Last Supper, explaining to the disciples that greatness is defined by service, not by merely exercising authority. Thus, we see that his death is to be understood as an absolute form of service, which itself demonstrates Jesus' true greatness. Later, as Jesus hangs on the cross, those around him taunt, "He saved others, let him save himself." The deep irony seen only with the eyes of faith is that by not simply saving himself Jesus did the will and work of God, which means the salvation of humankind.

Third, still in the context of the supper, Jesus teaches his disciples more extensively than in either Mark or Matthew. Indeed, Jesus' words show him to be a true prophet as he speaks of the future to those around him. Later, before Pilate, Jesus' adversaries accuse him of being a false prophet; thereafter, soldiers beat and mock Jesus, implying that he is no prophet at all. Again there is deep irony. The reader of Luke's account knows that Jesus can and does prophesy, for Simon Peter has denied Jesus exactly as Jesus said he would. Thus, those set against Jesus are shown themselves to be dishonest and blind.

Fourth, throughout this account Jesus, who goes to the cross, nevertheless acts with great authority. For example: (1) Foretelling Simon Peter's denials, Jesus informs him that Satan "demanded to sift all of you like wheat," but Jesus prayed for Peter, assuring his ultimate faithfulness which would allow him to strengthen his fellow disciples. (2) On the Mount of Olives, Jesus directs his disciples to prayer, in order that they may withstand temptation; and he himself engages in extraordinarily fervent praying. (3) At his arrest Jesus confronts Judas, rebukes his violent disciples, and confronts those who arrested him for their cowardly and satanic behavior. (4) In the courtyard of the house of the high priest Jesus observes Peter denying him, faces Peter when he fails, and himself stands steadfast in the face of deadly hostility despite the discouraging failure of all those around him. (5) In the council chamber Jesus defies his examiners, confronts them with their own faithlessness, and declares God's own verdict upon their actions. (6) Jesus stands in bold and majestic silence before Herod, and he says but little to Pilate. (7) On the road to the cross, Jesus consoles and warns the women who mourn him. (8) Crucified, Jesus prays for the forgiveness of those who murdered him in ignorance. (9) As he hangs upon the cross Jesus takes the abuse of those around him, even the abuse of a crucified criminal; and Jesus promises the other crucified criminal who speaks in his defense that he (the criminal) will join him (Jesus) in Paradise. Thus, dying he both forgives and saves. (10) At the moment of his death, Jesus quotes a line from Psalm 31 which shows his complete trust in God.

In sum, we find Luke's account styled to indicate the eschatological significance of the time. We learn that Jesus knows and makes provision for the faithfulness of his followers. And we see that Jesus' Passion was faithful obedience to the will of God, which brings the salvation of humanity.

Passion Sunday: The Celebration

For suggestions about the Passion/Palm Sunday liturgy, see the above commentary on Holy Week.

The hymn, "All Praise to Thee, for Thou, O King Divine," is a paraphrase of today's epistle, so where there is a concern about the length of the service, it may serve as a hymn or anthem connecting the Old Testament lesson to the reading of the Passion.

The reading of the Passion narrative may also be interpolated with hymns, but they should be appropriately chosen. See suggestions in the *New Handbook of the Christian Year,* p. 134.

It may be a bit overwhelming for the preacher to decide how to preach or what to preach about on this day when faced with such a marvelous array of scriptures from which to choose. If the reading of the Passion narrative has been well done, the preacher may feel it anticlimactic to say anything at all! Clearly, the sermon should be focused and to the point, rather than attempting to deal with every aspect of the Passion story in one presentation. The exegetical comment above will help isolate those elements that are particularly Lukan, so that the sermon can incorporate some of them in today's sermon.

The word *passion* itself will often present problems for the modern hearer who is more inclined to relate the word to tabloid headlines in the supermarket than to a church context. Today's sermon may seek to define passion as that kind of sacrificial, self-giving love that Jesus illustrates in Luke's Gospel. Here Jesus gives Peter positive assurance before he tells him that he will deny Christ. Jesus heals the ear of the high priest's slave. He forgives those who nail him to the cross, and he ushers a criminal into paradise.

A hymn too little known and used in the United States, but a fitting conclusion to Luke's rendering of the Passion, is Samuel Crossman's "My Song Is Love Unknown." It might be performed today as a solo at the offertory, but it would be helpful if the congregation were provided with a copy of the text. For words and music, see the Brethren and Mennonite *The Hymnal: A Worship Book,* no. 235; the Episcopal *The Hymnal 1982,* no. 458; the Lutheran *Book of Worship,* no. 94; *The Presbyterian Hymnal,* no. 76; and the *UCC Hymnal,* no. 74.

Holy Thursday

Old Testament Texts

Exodus 12:1-14 is one of the central descriptions of how and why the Passover is to be celebrated. Psalm 116:1-2, 12-19 celebrates the salvation of God as a rescue from death.

The Lesson: *Exodus 12:1-4 (5-10), 11-14*

The Passover

Setting. The confusion of the present form of Exodus 11–13 confronts any reader with immediate obstacles to interpretation. At least three different traditions have been brought together in these chapters (by at least two different hands) in order to describe what the salvific power of God is like. These three traditions include the death of the firstborn (Exodus 11; 12:12-13, 29-32; and perhaps 13:1, 11-16), the cultic celebration of Passover (Exodus 12:1-11, 21-27, 43-50) and unleavened bread or *massot* (Exodus 12:8, 14-20, 34; 13:3-10). It is not the task of a preacher to sort out the complex history of tradition in Exodus 11–13. It is a central task, however, for any interpreter of these texts to raise the question of why these (most likely) originally distinct traditions were brought together. An answer to this question will provide an interpretation of what salvation means. The limitation of the Old Testament lesson to Exodus 12:1-14 allows us to narrow the scope of this question down to the relationship between Passover and death of the firstborn, because the feast of unleavened bread is not central to these verses and occurs only in passing at v. 8.

Structure. The larger structure of Exodus 11–12 underscores the close relationship between the death of the firstborn and Passover. In

Exodus 11 God tells Moses that there is yet one final plague that will be brought upon the Egyptians—namely, the death of all first-born in the land. The reader is told in v. 7 that the result of this plague will be a visible distinction between Egyptians and Israelites. Exodus 12:1-14 immediately follows the divine prediction. In this text Moses prepares Israel for the night of destruction by telling them how they can be protected from the plague of death. The text can be outlined in the following manner.

I. The Instructions for the Passover (vv. 1-11)
   A. The time of the Passover
   B. The lamb
   C. The ritual
      1. Kill the lamb at evening
      2. Put blood on doorpost
      3. Eat the lamb in families
      4. Eat in haste
II. The Interpretation of the Passover (vv. 12-14)
   A. Death of firstborn
   B. The blood-sign for Israel
   C. The memorial

Significance. What is the relationship between the death of the firstborn and Passover, and how does this relationship provide insight into the meaning of salvation? The questions can best be answered first, by interpreting the death of the firstborn alone, and, second, by showing how the death of the firstborn is transformed when it is linked to the Passover.

When read independently, the death of the firstborn is a "we-they" story, or perhaps better an "us" against "them" story. The "them" are the Egyptians, whose firstborn are going to be killed by God, while the "us" are Israelites, whose firstborn are going to be just fine in the morning. This dichotomy is overly simplistic because the reader has been taken through a whole series of plagues in which Pharaoh has had ample time to avoid the plague of death. Neverthe-less, the end result of the death of the firstborn story, when it is read alone, is that ultimately the distinction between the people of God (the "us") and other humans (the "them") is something that is rooted in people themselves. The difference in the death of the firstborn is determined by whether a person's genetic structure is Egyptian or Israelite.

Second, the linking of Passover with the death of the firstborn necessarily complicates our understanding of (1) who is God and (2) who are the people of God. If the death of the firstborn gave the impression that God was dangerous only for certain groups of people and that the perilousness of God was, in fact, in service to the people of God (like a secret weapon), the linking of Passover underscores in no uncertain terms that God is dangerous for all persons, Israelites and Egyptians alike. The Passover instructions make it clear that God's plague of death will not discriminate between ethnic groups, and that only the blood of the lamb will save Israelites. Once our understanding of God is complicated with the addition of Passover, then it necessarily follows that our understanding of the people of God will also be changed. By underscoring that God is perilous for all in the Passover ritual, biblical writers are also saying that any distinction between the people of God and other humans must also lie outside of persons, which is, indeed, the case in the Passover ritual, where the distinction lies in the sacrificial blood. When Passover is linked to the death of the firstborn the reader learns that Israel is not saved because of ethnicity, nor even because they are oppressed, but because they participated in an atoning ritual that covered (or perhaps better, protected) them from the plague of death. Such an understanding of the people of God is implicitly universal, for there is nothing in the story to forbid an Egyptian from seeking the protection of the atoning blood. This insight forces a new reading of Exodus 11:7, for it suggests that only after the event of the death of the firstborn will we know who are the people of God—namely, those whose firstborn have survived because they participated in the atoning ritual.

The story of Passover goes against our modern sensibilities. Although the universal claims of salvation are more popular than ever in the contemporary church, we frequently root such claims in the belief that Christianity is a better way, and we look at advances in our own cultural setting as proof. The story of Passover argues for

the universal claims or promises of God's salvation in just the opposite way—namely, on the basis of universal sin. The story suggests
that if ethnicity or cultural context is to be the criteria for evaluating
God's salvation, then there is no such thing as a better way (or even
more likely, that the Egyptian way is better). Over against such
anthropological starting points for evaluating God's salvation, the
story presents a strong theology of sin in judging both Israel and
Egypt (the absence of blood on the doorpost will kill anyone), and it
is on the basis of this understanding of universal sin that a universal
promise of salvation is implied. There is nothing noble about the salvation of the Passover, for the first thing that any one waking up the
next morning must confront is blood dripping in their doorway.
There is no idealizing of their own cultural context here. The
imagery invites reflection on the nature of the Eucharist for Christians.

The Response: *Psalm 116:1-2, 12-19*

A Song of Thanksgiving

Setting. Psalm 116:1-2, 12-19 is a song of thanksgiving that looks
back on a wilderness experience from the perspective of someone
who has returned to the land of the living (v. 15).

Structure. Psalm 116 can be outlined into three parts: vv. 1-2 are a
call to praise with motivation for praise; vv. 3-9 recount the past
need of the psalm and God's response; vv. 12-19 recount a thank
offering as the result of a previous vow.

Significance. The call to praise with motivation in vv. 1-2 presents some textual problems. The opening statement "I love" in v. 1
lacks an object. The NRSV solution is probably the simplest. It
changes the syntax and makes "the Lord" the object. The verb tenses
are also not clear ("to hear" in v. 1 and "to call" in v. 2). They are
both imperfect, suggesting a present/future translation in English,
which does fit the context. The NRSV translates "to hear" in v. 1 as
past and "to call" in v. 2 as present/future. They might both be translated in the past, in which case the verb "to call" in v. 2 is not about
the psalmist's resolve to be faithful in the present/future, but a reference to a past call for help which is then described in vv. 3-6. This

87

latter translation underscores yet another problem in v. 2. The phrase in the NRSV, "as long as I live" is a loose paraphrase of the Hebrew "in my days," which is ambiguous and could have past or present/future meaning. At the very least the ambiguity in syntax and verb tenses gives the opening praise a sense of timelessness. The psalmist loves God not only because God has inclined his ear in the past (v. 2), but also because God will (continue to) hear his voice (v. 1).

Verses 3-6 shift momentarily to the past in order to describe a threatening situation of the psalmist. The imagery is graphic in v. 3. It is as though the psalmist was lassoed by the rope of death and corralled into Sheol. The tense then shifts into the present/future (the NRSV translates these verbs as past) to describe the experience of the psalmist ("I will find distress and grief") and how she will call on God in such situations ("I will call on the name of the Lord, 'O Lord, I beseech thee, save my life!' "). The shifting in verb tense frames the past situation in v. 3 more as a "typical" circumstance than as some nonrepeatable event. Thus it is easy for the psalmist to move from past event to the present confession in vv. 5-6, namely that God is merciful and gracious and can be counted on at all times for salvation. The insight of vv. 3-6 prompts exhortation and praise in vv. 7-9. The psalmist exhorts herself to faithfulness in v. 7, and then addresses God directly for the first time in v. 8 with a mixture of praise and confession, "For you have delivered my soul from death. . . . " This section comes to an end in v. 9 with the present/future confession that the psalmist walks in the presence of God in the land of the living. The final two sections of vv. 12-15 and 16-19 present thank offerings to God in light of the experience of salvation.

New Testament Texts

The readings focus on the Lord's Supper and the Last Supper respectively. Paul reminds his readers that the final meal that Jesus celebrated with his disciples is commemorated and reenacted in the worship of the Church as a bold eschatological proclamation of the cross and its consequences. John neither narrates the meal nor recalls any words of institution spoken by Jesus, rather the supper is remembered as the context in which Jesus taught his disciples in deed and word about the real meaning of his ministry, which was defined in terms of selfless service and sacrificial love.

The Epistle: *I Corinthians 11:23-26*

Pondering the Lord's Supper

Setting. We last encountered I Corinthians in the readings for the Third Sunday in Lent, and the reader may consult the comments there on setting for a broad introduction to the epistle. Our reading comes in the eleventh chapter of the letter, a section interested in orderly worship and the faithful maintenance of tradition in the practices of church. In 11:17-34 Paul is particularly concerned with the observance of the Lord's Supper in the context of the assembly of the congregation.

As the Corinthians gathered, apparently it was their practice to take a common meal and in that setting to celebrate the Lord's Supper (either in the course of the eating or at the conclusion of the meal). Problems existed, however, because of the diverse social classes from which the members of the congregation came. The wealthy members were dining lavishly to the humiliation of the poorer congregants. Paul's fuller comments, within the course of which the verses of our reading occur, aims at correcting the divisive situation.

Structure. Paul reminds the Corinthians of a tradition concerning the Lord's Supper in these verses. Verse 23*a* formally introduces the tradition which he recalls in vv. 23*b*-25. Then, in v. 26 Paul interprets the celebration of the Lord's Supper. Thus, we find the recognition of tradition, the memory of the Last Supper and Jesus' words of institution over the bread and the cup, and a pointed statement about the meaning of the celebration of the Lord's Supper in the life of the Church.

Significance. The story of the Lord's Supper clearly belongs to the sacred memory of the Church. That memory lives as the teachers and preachers in the Church carefully pass the tradition on to others. Paul stands in the line of transmission, having both received and passed on the sacred teaching; and his words to the Corinthians show that he understands this tradition to have originated with "the Lord"—thus, the authority and importance of the teaching.

As Paul retells the Corinthians of the tradition of the Lord's Supper, he locates the origin of the practice in the context of Jesus' Passion. The words "on the night when he was betrayed" recall the terrible ignominy that the Lord suffered. Then, in speaking of the bread Paul recalls that Jesus said his body was broken "for you," so that the suffering and shame of the Passion are shown to have been endured as an act of grace for humanity.

Furthermore, Paul reports that the commandment to celebrate the Lord's Supper ("do this") came from the Lord himself. The celebration of the Supper is, therefore, the Lord's and not merely the Church's own activity. Indeed, the celebration of the Supper is to be oriented toward the Lord, in his honor, as is clear from the words "in remembrance of me."

As Paul continues by referring to the tradition concerning the cup, we find that the celebration is founded in the creation of the "new covenant." The idea of a "new covenant" relates to Jeremiah 31:31, where one finds that God's people are called out and transformed by the presence and power of God at work among them. From the tradition we learn that this new covenant is established or sealed in Jesus' blood—that is, the price paid for redefining or reestablishing a right relationship between God and humanity was offered by Jesus' himself in compliance with the will and work of God. In turn, the words "as often as you do it" inform us that there is no other way to celebrate the Lord's Supper than in recognition and gratitude for the grace of God at work in Jesus Christ.

Interpreters debate whether v. 26 is part of the tradition that Paul received or Paul's own commentary. The statement could not easily go back to the Lord himself in its present form, although it has some resemblance to Mark 14:25; Matthew 26:29; and Luke 22:16. Whatever the origin of the statement, we learn from this verse that the celebration of the Lord's Supper is not simply a recollection of the past, even the past as a saving act of God. Indeed, here we see that the Lord's Supper orients us toward the future—that is, toward the Lord's future. As the past makes provision for our present existence, so the future lays claim on our lives right now. In the life of the Church the proper memory and practice of the Lord's Supper is itself dramatic proclamation of the significance of the work of God in Jesus Christ. We celebrate the cross, but also the ultimate triumph of God, a reality that those in Christ already experience, but for the full form of which we eagerly await.

The Gospel: *John 13:1-7, 31b-35*

Seeing and Hearing the New Commandment of Christ

Setting. Verse 1 signals that we have moved out of the so-called Book of Signs (John 1–12) and into the so-called Book of Glory (13–20 [21?]) with the overt statement that Jesus recognized that his "hour" had come, and, furthermore, the supernatural significance of the time is signaled by the report concerning the activity of "the devil" in this context (v. 2).

It is the day before Passover, and Jesus and his disciples take a meal together. During or after the meal Jesus washed the disciples' feet. Conversation on washing, humility, and love followed, along with Jesus' troubled prediction that Judas would betray him. Jesus dismissed Judas from the gathering, and when he had gone Jesus began to speak to the disciples. After a brief exchange with Simon Peter, Jesus eventually spoke at great length to his followers.

Structure. Two units of material form our lesson. Verses 1-7 move the Gospel's story into the time of Jesus' "hour," telling of the meal and of Jesus' washing the disciples' feet. Then, the lectionary suggests taking a leap over the ensuing conversation, prediction, and dismissal of Judas. With this move, we come in vv. 31b-35 to Jesus' initial words to his disciples, prior to the exchange with Peter and the lengthy "last discourses." Thus, our lesson brings us in a moment of utmost importance to Jesus' action and words to his disciples, both of which are designed to reveal the nature of true ministry and true community in love.

Significance. Regarding the date of the last meal and the absence of Jesus' words over the bread and the cup, one should consult a full-blown commentary in preparation for worship. These matters are not treated here, but some perceptive member of the congregation is sure to see the distinctiveness of this account in relation to the account(s) in the Synoptic Gospels; so be prepared. (The treatment by R. E. Brown in the Anchor Bible [*The Gospel According to John* (Garden City, N.Y.: Doubleday, 1970) pp. 548-614] covers nearly every possible question, regardless of one's confessional affiliation, in an encyclopedic fashion.)

The sequence in the first part of our lesson is action, question, and enigmatic reply. The narrative is symbolic, although Jesus' reply to Peter indicates that without further information—given in the account of Jesus' Passion that follows—real comprehension is not possible. Thus, the story itself demands that we throw the net wide in reflecting upon this event.

The lowly service that Jesus renders in washing the disciples' feet is a prefiguration of the crucifixion itself. The washing of the disciples' feet and Christ's death on the cross are analogous in terms of the humility, service, and cleansing inherent in both; and both acts are rooted in divine love. Jesus' action in washing the disciples' feet is a telling symbol of the crucifixion—that is, a gracious act of God that purifies humanity as it calls us to faith. In turn, the cross and the footwashing set a standard of genuine humility that we are called to imitate as disciples of Christ. John opens this section of the Gospel by telling us that Jesus had not only loved his disciples, but he demonstrated that he loved them to the very end—meaning that at all costs, even and especially death, Jesus loved his own.

In the second section of the lesson, Jesus declares the "hour": "Now the Son of Man has been glorified, and God has been glorified in him" (v. 31). In turn, Jesus tells the disciples plainly that the task he leaves them is that they demonstrate to the world that they are his disciples by manifesting the same love among themselves that he embodied in washing their feet (and, even more, in dying on the cross).

Jesus' opening words about glory tie together his being glorified by God and God's being glorified in him, both of which are related to Jesus' loving and exact obedience to the will of God. In other words, the glory of God was plainly displayed in Jesus Christ. What does this mean? As we see Jesus selflessly give his very life for his disciples, we see the depths of the love of God, which is indeed the substance of God's glory. Love characterizes the person of God, and for humans who are in fellowship with God, love is to characterize the life they live among themselves. Love here is not to be reduced to a sentiment or a feeling, rather it is the will to will the well-being of others at all costs to one's self. We are told that God has this capacity, and in Jesus Christ we are called to experience that love so that we ourselves become capable of embodying the same love.

Despite the beauty of this story and the poetic quality of Jesus' words, this striking lesson is a challenge for preaching. The point is at once simple and complex. The sermon should treat at least these themes: The love of God is manifested in Jesus Christ; that love is God's own glory; as Jesus' disciples we benefit from that selfless love; and as Jesus' disciples we are called to manifest that love ourselves. The images of footwashing and the cross are appropriate for developing the proclamation.

Holy Thursday: The Celebration

The richness of liturgical and homiletical possibilities for this day can be overwhelming, so preachers and worship planners need to be very clear about what they intend to do within the time they have available, in order that the congregation be not overstimulated to the point of anxiety or overwhelmed by the array of images and references coming at it. It may be helpful to list as many of the options as possible and then ask what is practical in each particular setting. Different options might be used from year to year.

> Parish Meal leading to the Lord's Supper
> Old Testament Reading of the Passover
> New Testament Reading of the Lord's Supper
> Gospel Reading of the Washing of Feet
> Sermon (interpreting one or more of the lessons)
> The Rite of Washing of Feet
> The Lord's Supper
> Stripping of the Altar
> Prayer Vigil until Midnight

The parish meal prior to the evening service is suggested by the Passover model of the Synoptic Gospels. It is standard practice in Church of the Brethren congregations to observe the Lord's Supper within the context of a parish meal, which also includes the washing of feet. The whole service (except the stripping of the altar and the prayer vigil) could take place in the parish hall around tables. This assumes that the hall is of sufficient size to accommodate the congregation. The appropriateness of some liturgical acts may need to be determined by such practical considerations of the number of people involved and the physical environment.

Although the parish meal may be modeled on the Passover account, Christians should be discouraged from doing their own version of the Passover meal. This act is sometimes considered an affront to our Jewish brothers and sisters, and it suggests that we have not understood clearly enough that for Christians the Lord's Supper is our Passover meal. Congregations that wish to learn more about the spirit of Judaism and the place the Seder plays in Jewish self-understanding should enter into a dialogue with Jews in the local community and, as a part of that dialogue, accept invitations to be guests at Seder meals. That will preserve the authenticity of the Seder and it can help prevent unnecessary interfaith misunderstandings.

The ceremony of foot washing is one of those events that should be carefully considered in terms of the congregation and the environment. In some traditions, it is a precious part of their community life. Other congregations will perceive it as a cultural anachronism or a liturgical period piece. The Holy Week introduction above suggests one alternative to foot washing. Some congregations do the service prior to the evening Eucharist, so that those who do not wish to participate will not seem to be excluded. In other congregations, only twelve members are chosen to have their feet washed by the pastor.

Two hymns that have been making their appearance in recent hymnals are particularly fitting to accompany the rite of foot washing. One dates back to the eighth century, "Where Charity and Love Prevail." The other is a contemporary text set to a folk tune from Ghana, "Jesu, Jesu." These will also serve as sermon hymns if the primary text is from John.

Although the Last Supper is the paramount image informing this night's Eucharist, it should be remembered that we are recalling that night, not playacting it, and that it is still the Lord's Supper, the meal with the Risen Christ, that we are observing. The use of the older, more penitential language may have special meaning for many in this particular service.

The Holy Week introduction above describes one pattern for the stripping of the altar. Although the use of Tenebrae has become popular in many churches as a conclusion to the Maundy Thursday service, its use is questionable because, rather than leading the people to anticipate Good Friday, it rehearses both it and Easter Day. It jumps the gun, as it were, and races towards Easter without giving the time to Good Friday that is called for. There were, after all, reasons why the Roman Catholics who invented Tenebrae abandoned it when they initiated the Holy Week reforms. The conclusion of the Maundy Thursday service should be a preparation for and entrance into the Good Friday liturgy.

Other congregations have found an increase of devotion by encouraging persons to maintain a vigil of prayer in the church at least until midnight as a form of remembering the agony of Christ in the garden. Appropriate materials could be made available as a guide for prayer and meditation.

EASTER: CREATION'S EIGHTH DAY

Although Easter is the central, formative event in the Christian revelation, and although it is the day of the largest attendance of the faithful at church, it frequently has an anticlimactic character after all of the emphasis put into Lent. Easter Day, the day toward which the Lenten solemnity has been directed, ends up marking both the high point in the year's attendance and the beginning of the downward spiral toward the summer low point.

This may be because Easter is finally mystery, a wonderfully overwhelming mystery, and the human creature cannot for long bear what it cannot understand. We are familiar with the miracle of birth, and so we concur with the sentiment that Christmas should be kept all the year long. I have seen men and women leave the church weeping after the solemn stripping of the altar on Maundy Thursday, because we know what it is to have rejoicing turned into mourning, to surrender the brightness of life to the shadow of death. Maybe that is why Easter is so unbearable: it dares to proclaim a reality opposed to that which we experience in the natural realm. We hear no one suggesting that we keep Easter all the year long, even though the observance of the Lord's Day every seven days intends precisely that!

The Christian year and lectionary seek to make us aware that Easter is more than one day in the year and to restore the historic observance of the Great Fifty Days, the time from Easter Day through the Day of Pentecost. No longer do we speak of Sundays "after Easter," but "of Easter," reminding us that the celebration is an ongoing event in the Church's life of prayer and proclamation. Pentecost is not the first day of a new season; it is the last day of the

Easter festival, uniting the events of the Resurrection and the empowerment of the Church. The Great Fifty Days are observed as a unity because they are presented that way in the Lukan chronology. In John's Gospel, the risen Lord breathes the Holy Spirit upon the apostles on the evening of Easter Day. The Christian year achieves a kind of liturgical harmonization of the Gospels by placing the Day of Pentecost in the evening of the season. The observance of sacred time thus helps teach us that the Resurrection, the Ascension, and the gift of the Spirit are mutually dependent events participating in the same theological reality. Each presupposes the others.

It has not been unknown in the history of Christian preaching for the Easter proclamation to lose its radical character and for the theological center to be ignored in the interest of making the day more palatable to modern sensibilities. This began early in the English-speaking world, since the day was called "Easter," after the pagan goddess of spring, rather than some form of the word *Pasch,* which was the practice in the Romance languages. Pagan symbolism has frequently dominated the observance and turned it into a kind of vernal rite, complete with the fertility images of eggs and rabbits. Spring symbolism has ended up as the content of the Easter message, and Resurrection is reduced to a biological necessity, a regeneration of the earth, while we rejoice in our hymns that "Flowers make glee among the hills, / And set the meadows dancing"! It is salutary for those of us in the northern hemisphere to remember that in half the world Easter occurs in the autumn.

The other way in which the radical proclamation of Easter has often been compromised has been through substituting a platonic doctrine of the immortality of the soul for the biblical concept of resurrection. Eternal life is seen as something we have a "right" to rather than the free gift of God in Jesus Christ. To the degree that we are immortal, it is in relation to what God has done in salvation rather than creation. That salvation is the cause for our Easter proclamation and celebration.

As Lent has dealt with the issue of mortality, beginning with Ash Wednesday, so now Easter celebrates that immortality which is God's gift, the antidote to sin's poison. The Easter Vigil has been restored in the practice of many churches because it presents in a unified fashion the story of sin and salvation in the lessons and applies that story through baptism to the life of the individual believer who is made a part of the Body of Christ and is nourished spiritually at the Lord's Table. Pastors and worship committees unfamiliar with the Vigil should consult the *New Handbook of the Christian Year* to find a copy of the service and helpful commentary about it.

Many preachers and worship leaders are dismayed when first they look at the list of lessons for the Vigil and the length of the service. At this point of fatigue we need to remember that the liturgy was made for us and not we for the liturgy. Without endorsing some kind of liturgical minimalism, it is possible to ask what is reasonable for a congregation that is underexposed to this particular tradition, and to ask what is most important within this service.

Historically, the Vigil was the time for the baptism of those who had received instruction and their participation for the first time in the Lord's Supper. The reading of the history of salvation lasted through the night, leading to the baptism, the illumination, of the converts as the sun began to rise and they were buried and raised with Christ in baptism. This intricate interweaving of story and song, light and darkness, water and oil, touching and being touched, bread and wine, is eloquent testimony to the Church's understanding of the liturgy as a multimedia event!

For churches locked into an hour time frame, it is obvious that the Vigil in its fullness will have difficulty gaining acceptance. Pastors might wish to think of spreading the components of the Vigil out over a period of time. This maintains the sequence of events in their integrity, and as they move through the Sundays of Easter they help the congregation focus on the Paschal mystery throughout the season.

The four sections of the Vigil (Light, Word, Water, Eucharist) may be divided among the first three Sundays of Easter by doing the service of light as part of the traditional sunrise service, the service of the Word as the "regular service" on Easter Day, the administration of baptism on the Second Sunday of Easter when we are reminded in the lesson from Revelation that we have been freed from our sins by the blood of Christ, and the Lord's Supper on the

Third Sunday of Easter when the Gospel reading recalls the meal on the seashore with the risen Lord. The Fourth through the Seventh Sundays of Easter may then be devoted to what has been called "mystagogical catechesis," training in the meaning of these sacred mysteries in which we have participated. Commentary on the lessons of the Vigil will be found in *Year A: Lent/Easter* in this commentary series.

Baptism is central to our celebration of Easter, and Easter is central to our understanding of baptism. The Lord's Day is the eighth day of creation, the day of the new creation brought into being by Christ's victory over death. In a time when baptism is the center of so much theological discussion and controversy, pastors and people might do well to explore and experience the meaning of baptism from a liturgical perspective rather than to argue about meaning in terms of static, academic categories.

This may mean "saving up" baptisms for Easter, so that there will be individuals ready to receive the Easter sacrament. This in itself testifies to an understanding of baptism which mantains that it is not an individualistic rite, but a community one. The baptisms might be spread across the Great Fifty Days. This allows some convenience in timing, but it also emphasizes the meaning of the whole season. More than one baptism should be done at a time whenever possible, however, so as not to lose the communal nature of the event.

The renewal of baptismal vows is a part of many Vigil services, especially if there are no baptisms to be administered, but if there is no Vigil, as with other components mentioned above, it may find an independent place as one of the Sunday services of the season. The major service of Easter Day itself is preferable, since the renewal service can be a vivid reminder of what brings everyone, the regulars and the one-timers, together in the Christian family. A brief form of baptismal renewal may be used for the rest of the Sundays of Easter at the beginning of the service as part of the entrance rite and in place of the confession of sin, as follows:

Alleluia! Christ is risen.
The Lord is risen indeed. Alleluia!
Let us pray.
God of the Covenants,

we thank you for this gift of water
which gives fruitfulness to the fields
and refreshment and cleansing to your creatures.
Water witnessed to your goodness
when you led your people through the sea
and satisfied their thirst from flinty rock.
You consecrated your Son
in the waters of the Jordan,
and through water
you have given us a new birth from above.
May this water remind us of our baptism,
and let us share the joy
of all who have been baptized this Easter.
We ask this in the name of the Risen Christ. **Amen.**

Sprinkling water towards the people, the minister says:

Remember your baptism and be thankful.

*The service continues with the opening hymn.**

Baptisms are possibly the most ecumenically segregated events in the Christian Church. The sign act that is understood to incorporate us into the catholic Church is most often observed in congregational isolation. Easter can be a time to realize the fullness of the sign by administering baptism in company with other congregations so that its ecumenical character is realized. This can easily be done when two or more churches celebrate the Easter Vigil together.

*Based on a prayer for the blessing of water in *With All God's People: The New Ecumenical Prayer Cycle—Orders of Service,* John Carden, ed. (Geneva: World Council of Churches, 1989), p. 110.

Second Sunday of Easter

Old Testament Texts

Acts 5:27-32 is an account of Peter and the other apostles before the high priest. Psalm 150 is a hymn of praise.

The Lesson: *Acts 5:27-32*

Bloodguilt and Obedience

Setting. Acts 5:27-32 is part of a larger story that includes at least vv. 17-26. Verses 17-26 narrate the arrest of the disciples for teaching and healing in the Temple and their miraculous escape with the aid of an angel. The setting of the lectionary text, therefore, is of the disciples before the Jewish leaders. As the exchange between the high priest and Peter indicates, this is the second such confrontation, with the first occurring in Acts 4.

Structure. The lectionary text separates into two or three parts. If the focus is on the speakers, then it clearly divides between the high priest's speech in vv. 27-28 and Peter's reply in vv. 29-32. The content of the text suggests three parts, with the speech of the high priest in vv. 27-28 and a two-part speech by Peter: a proclamation about Jesus in vv. 29-31 and a confession of apostolic witness in v. 32.

Significance. The tone of the exchange between Peter and the high priest is sharp. As noted this is the second confrontation between Jewish leaders and the apostles, and it would appear that Luke is building the tension between the Temple and the early church to prepare for the mission to the Gentiles. Luke sets the tone of confrontation by the way in which he has constructed the question of the high priest in v. 28. The first part of the statement recounts the earlier command in 4:18 that the apostles not speak in the name of Jesus. The link between the two speeches is so close that the name of Jesus is absent in 5:28. The second part of the question, however, states the substance of the confrontation, when the high priest accuses the disciples of bringing bloodguilt on them for the death of Jesus. Bloodguilt means that the blood of a murdered person requires compensation (see for example Deuteronomy 19:10). The issues surrounding bloodguilt are certainly judicial, but they are also theological. Because blood was considered to contain or embody life in some way, it was invested with a mystical power, which if shed by means of murder demanded compensation—if from no one else, then eventually from God. Note, for example, how the blood of Abel takes on personality in Genesis 4:10 after Cain kills him, which prompts God to take on the role of an avenger, "Listen; your brother's blood is crying out to me from the ground!" Both the judicial and the theological aspects of bloodguilt are most likely present in the statement of the high priest.

Peter's response in vv. 29-32 separates into two topics: vv. 30-31 address the theological aspect of bloodguilt and vv. 29 and 32 focus on obedience. First bloodguilt in vv. 30-31. The language throughout is sharp and confrontational. Luke has Peter make the startling accusation that the Jewish leaders killed Jesus, and, given the preceding speech, this must be interpreted as bloodguilt. The point here is less an accusation of guilt than a proclamation of salvation in Jesus. A careful look at the syntax of the speech will provide illustration. Peter's speech consists of two central points about God: God raised Jesus and God exalted Jesus to be Leader and Savior. The content of these two designations (Leader and Savior) is spelled out with two specific actions at the close of v. 31: Jesus gives repentance to Israel and forgiveness of sins. Stated simply, the result is that Jesus ends bloodguilt, which goes to the very core of what divine forgiveness means. Second, obedience in vv. 29 and 32. The proclamation about the cessation of bloodguilt is framed by the motif of obedience. In v. 29 Peter explains why he and the other apostles have continued to preach in the name of Jesus by stating that they must obey God and not humans. The motif of obedience then returns at the close of his speech in v. 32, when Peter links the Holy Spirit (which is the primary power revealing that Jesus ends bloodguilt) with those who obediently follow God.

Two themes are important for preaching this text. If the focus is on the Jewish leaders, then the primary message is salvation. Luke has placed this message of salvation in a highly confrontational setting. A subordinate reason for the confrontation is to prepare the reader for the larger mission to the Gentiles, which begins within a few chapters in the book of Acts. Thus there is a sociological aspect for Luke in the confrontation between apostles and Jewish leaders. Unfortunately sociology has often become the primary focus of this text, which has given rise to anti-semitism, itself a form of Christian bloodguilt. The primary reason for the confrontation is theological, and here the point of the text has nothing to do with Jewish-Christian relations, but with God's relationship to us. Luke has created a confrontational text that is extreme in its accusations in order to explore the nature of salvation around the theme of bloodguilt. His primary message is that Jesus ends any bloodguilt between God and us. His second message is that if the focus is on the apostles then the primary message is obedience. Those who know what God has done in Christ, and are now filled with the power of the Holy Spirit, are called to do two things in this text: theologically, they must proclaim the power of the gospel by using the name of Jesus and, sociologically, not practice bloodguilt.

The Response: *Psalm 150*

A Hymn of Praise

Setting. Psalm 150 is certainly a hymn of praise. Its tone is exuberant. Yet upon closer reflection it is peculiar in that no ground or reason for praise is given, as is normal in a praise hymn, with such lines as, "Praise God *because* of . . ." or "Praise God *for* he. . . ." Psalm 150 is simply a series of calls to praise.

Structure. One could argue that there is no structure to the psalm, in which case it is simply a thirteen-part call to praise. The content of the hymn does suggest a three-part movement consisting of instruction concerning where to praise God (vv. 1-2), how to praise God (vv. 3-5), and who should praise God (v. 6).

Significance. Verses 1-2 designated the sanctuary as the location for praising God. It is the place where heaven and earth meet, hence the location of the firmament (v. 1), and it is the place where the mighty acts of God in the past are made known (v. 2). The litany of instruments in vv. 3-5 emphasize the important role of music in worship as a means for praising God. Finally, v. 6 makes it clear that all life must praise God.

New Testament Texts

The texts for this Sunday treat the theme of the resurrection of Christ in remarkably different ways. The passage from Revelation revels in a panorama of themes, including the Resurrection, to tell of the wonder of God's grace. The lesson from John recounts a series of incidents (briefly, but giving many important details) to celebrate the season of Easter.

The Epistle: *Revelation 1:4-8*

God's Grace and Peace Through Jesus Christ

Setting. The book of Revelation is a remarkable early Christian writing. It is a fitting final document for the New Testament (and the Bible), for it testifies to that which is anticipated in all that went before—namely, the ultimate triumph of God. The work comprises three literary types. Predominantly, Revelation is a piece of apocalyptic literature, but worked into this kind of writing are epistles (chapters 2 and 3) and several prophetic-style declarations (part of our lesson!). Discerning the style in which a section is written assists greatly in interpreting the various parts of the whole.

The verses of our lesson come after the title and introductory statement at the outset of Revelation (vv. 1-3). Remarkably, our lesson casts the beginning of Revelation in the form of the opening of typical Hellenistic letter, a style well-known from the epistles of the New Testament.

Structure. The standard beginning of a Hellenistic letter had three parts: (1) salutation—sender to recipient; (2) greeting—in a word, phrase, or sentence(s); and (3) thanksgiving—often with religious tones. Our text is an elaborate, highly religious form of the latter two parts of this manner of opening a letter. The salutation occurs in v. 4*a*; then, the greeting comes in vv. 4*b*-5*a*; and a complex thanksgiving fills out vv. 5*b*-8. The thanksgiving itself combines a polished doxology (vv. 5*b*-6), a prophetic word concerning the coming of Jesus Christ (v. 7), and a "word-of-God" in direct speech (v. 8).

Significance. It is difficult to imagine more doctrinal and confessional material being packed into four verses of scripture than we find in this lesson. A careful look at the passage reveals themes and structures that are highly suggestive for proclamation.

First, v. 4*a* gives us an awareness of who the author and recipients are. This is important for understanding the content of the following lines. The author is John, an early Christian leader who was exiled to the island of Patmos during a period of opposition or persecution of the church in Asia Minor. The seven churches mentioned are named explicitly in a series of letters to the individual congregations in Revelation 2–3. Problems existed in these congregations because of the difficulties being experienced—suffering brought anxiety, doubts, and laxity.

Second, the greeting will seem familiar, for in a style similar to Paul's, John pronounces "grace" and "peace" upon those reading Revelation. This grace and peace are specifically associated with God and Jesus Christ. Several items here merit attention. God is named in such a way that the reader ponders God's eternal character and majesty over all. Taken in the context of the whole of Revelation, however, these ascriptions are more than statements or recognitions of God's temporal infinity and omnipotence; these descriptions imply God's dependability and capacity to care for those in need. In turn, Jesus Christ is named in a three-fold ascription. He is called "faithful witness," a reference to his life and ministry, especially to his Passion and death. He is called "the firstborn of the dead," an unmistakable reference to his Resurrection. And, he is called "the ruler of kings on earth," a recognition of his exaltation and Lordship. From this God and from this Jesus Christ, John speaks of grace and peace. Interpreters often explain that grace is the nature of God's saving work in Jesus Christ and that peace is the result of God's saving actions. In combinations with the ways John names God and Jesus Christ, we may also think of grace as God's nature or character and peace as God's goal in relation to humanity.

Third, the doxological pronouncements at the conclusion of the thanksgiving are more than lofty phrases heaped on the greeting like frosting on a cake. In the initial christological doxology we learn of the meaning of the work of Jesus Christ. The phrase "by his blood" indicates that John is offering an interpretation of the significance of the death of Jesus. It occurred for us out of Christ's love, and it gives us the freedom from our sins that grants us the peace that God desires for us. The statement is confessional, not explanatory. Moreover, the result of this freedom is that humanity is constituted as a "kingdom"—that is, the locus of the lordship of God, where God's will is supreme. And John says those whom he addresses (Christians) are "priests"—that is, there is an equality in Christian faith that supersedes cultic ritual that distinguishes some persons as closer to God than others.

In turn, we hear of Jesus Christ's coming. The language of v. 7 employs words, phrases, and images related to the "day of the Lord"—that is, a day appointed by God on which the denizens of this world will be judged. As always in such eschatological passages, we are reminded that God through Christ rules the future, and the demand that God's standards regulate our lives is registered with force.

Finally, John reports God's own words. The phrase "Alpha and Omega" refers to the first and last letters of the Greek alphabet, so that God is "everything from A to Z." This inclusive "omni-image" refers back to the manner of naming God in the greeting (v. 4b) and even picks up the doxological language at the end of v. 6. The title applied here to God, "Almighty" (*pantocrator*), recognizes that God is indeed "Lord" of all.

This compact, complex epistolary opening informs John's readers (and us!) who God is, who Jesus Christ is, what God has done and is doing and will do in Jesus Christ, and reminds them (and us!) that God's work in Jesus Christ places a claim on our lives. We are freed, but we are free for a purpose, and God through Christ evaluates our lives. This declaration is more promise than threat, being meant to encourage those in difficulty to trust in God despite difficulties.

The Gospel: *John 20:19-31*

Peace, Commission, Doubts, Blessing, and Belief

Setting. After the Passion narrative of John's Gospel (from the garden to the grave) the story of God's work through Jesus Christ pauses briefly as the characters in the story observe the Sabbath. Then, with the Sabbath having created a disjunction in the account, we move to the first day of the week (Sunday) and rejoin the story by following the activities of Mary Magdalene and certain of Jesus' disciples. After the account of Jesus' appearance to Mary in the garden, we come to the appearance stories in our lesson for this week.

Structure. This lesson contains three items: two distinct but related scenes and a formal word of closure related to everything that has come before in the Gospel. First, vv. 19-23 recount the appearance of the risen Jesus to the disciples as they were gathered behind closed doors on the evening of the first Easter. Then, building off this account, vv. 24-29 tell of Thomas's absence from among the disciples when Jesus originally appeared, of his doubts, and of Jesus' subsequent appearance to him in the presence of the other disciples. Finally, vv. 30-31 make what is surely one of the finest closing statements ever offered for a book (except the Gospel does not conclude here!).

Significance. The presence of the risen Lord comes in a miraculous manner and grants to the disciples the "peace" of the Lord. There is no rebuke because of the fear that has paralyzed the disciples and driven them into hiding. Instead of a negative tone the appearance is purely positive in character; it means and brings peace. The reaction of the disciples is appropriate, they are overjoyed at the sight of the risen Jesus. Their joy is far more than a static or selfish experience, which means only good feelings; it is the disposition to which Christ issues a commission to service. The good news of the reality of Christ's resurrection, the overpowering revelation of the irrepressible nature of the love of God, is the foundation of a divine call to faithful service. Christ commissions the disciples, making of them real Christians—a term that in its origin meant "little Christs." As God sent Jesus, so now the risen Lord

Jesus Christ sends the disciples to do the will and the work of God in the world. As the light of the world Christ came into darkness. Though in the death of Jesus it appeared that darkness had overcome the light, now through the Resurrection we are shown that the light still shines in the darkness. Indeed, the light that shines calls forth new "points of light" as Christ calls the disciples into the same kind of divinely directed service that he had given his whole self to do. Yet, notice here, as is ever the case in relation to the gospel's call to service, the disciples (and we) are not merely told to get the job done. The disciples (and we) are given the powerful gift of the Holy Spirit. We receive God's own power and presence for doing the work to which our risen Lord Jesus Christ directs us.

In the next scene we find that reasonable doubts do not disqualify us for discipleship. Instead our doubts are addressed by the risen Lord who alone is capable of allaying our apprehensions. Today there are many who share Thomas's reservations. Many would insist that the favor granted to Thomas gave him an unfair advantage, for who would not believe after having seen the risen Lord. It is well, however, to reflect carefully in relation to this text. While we do not share Thomas's seeming advantage, we also do not have the serious handicap that confounded his capacity to believe the good news that Christ is risen. We have never known Christ in the flesh. We have never seen him crucified, dead, and buried; and today we live in a world where for nearly two thousand years believers have been sustained by their conviction of the reality of the Resurrection and of Christ's real presence in their lives. For us the reality of lives of faith are as much evidence of Christ's presence as was his standing before Thomas in the company of the other disciples after they had known him crucified. Yet, be that as it may, in this lesson Christ's own words are spoken through the text to us as a word of sacred assurance, "Blessed are those who have not seen and yet have come to believe."

As the twentieth chapter of John comes to its conclusion (perhaps recording the ending of an earlier edition of the Gospel—see other commentaries) the author turns directly to the readers and states the purposes of his writing. The stories in John's Gospel are testimony to the work of God in Jesus Christ, and they are offered to inspire faith in Jesus Christ. In turn, that faith means life in his name for those who believe.

Easter 2: The Celebration

Because the Gospel reading is the same on "Low Sunday" for all three years of the lectionary cycle, the reader is referred to the Celebration entries in the previous volumes.

The lesson from Revelation gives rise to more liturgical and homiletical considerations than its brevity would suggest. The first part of the lesson can serve as the day's form of greeting to the congregation:

Grace to you and peace from the One who is and who was and who is to come;
      or
Grace to you and peace from Jesus Christ, the faithful witness, the firstborn of the dead, and the ruler of the rulers of the earth.

Either of the above function well as a Greeting or Call to Worship because they establish the church's agenda in the church's language, as opposed to the secular world's "Good Morning." The language of the Greeting should make clear that the worship time and place is devoted in a special way to the service of God by those people who have been loved by God, freed from their sins, and made a priestly society under the rule of God (Revelation 1:5-6). It has been suggested that if our calls to worship cannot get beyond "Good Morning," then our benedictions ought to be, "Have a nice day."

Revelation 1:5b-6 ("To him who loves us . . .") is referred to as an ascription of praise. These are sometimes confused with benedictions and used in their place, the most notorious example being the conclusion of the previous book, Jude 24-25. A benediction is supposed to pronounce a word of blessing upon the people and is addressed to them; an ascription of praise is a doxological utterance about the glory, majesty, and power of God. Ascriptions of praise have been traditionally used to conclude the sermon if a brief prayer is not used. They are to be preferred over the use of the word *amen* by the preacher, since *amen* expresses agreement, and we assume that the preacher agrees with what he or she has said! The "amen" should not be degraded to the function of a clue to let the people know when the sermon is over.

Revelation 1:7 is the source for the great Wesley hymn, "Lo, He Comes with Clouds Descending," which many hymnals assign to the Advent repertoire. "Rejoice, the Lord is King" was written by Wesley originally as an Easter text, and it would fit well with today's reading from Revelation.

The use of the term *pantocrator* (see commentary above) calls to mind the iconographic traditions of Eastern Orthodoxy in which the depiction of Christ as pantocrator plays a major role. Icons or reproductions that portray Christ Pantocrator might be displayed in the church today and/or for the rest of the season. Such an icon might also be featured on the bulletin cover.

Although it may seem unnecessary to mention this, experience dictates otherwise. Readers of the lesson for today and the Sundays following should be reminded that it is the Revelation of St. John and not Revelations.

The references to peace in Revelation and the Gospel reading suggest that the Peace as a liturgical action following the confession of sin or before the offering would be appropriate.

Third Sunday of Easter

Old Testament Texts

Acts 9 is the account of Saul's confrontation with Jesus on the road to Damascus. Psalm 30 is a hymn of thanksgiving.

The Lesson: *Acts 9:1-6 (7-20)*

Saul Meets Jesus, and Ananias Answers the Call

Setting. The apostle Paul is introduced as Saul, the persecutor of the church, in Acts 7:58–8:3 through two actions, first, as the person who held the coats while Stephen was stoned, and, second, as one of the foremost persecutors of Christians in Jerusalem. The storyline of Saul stops for the remainder of Acts 8 while Luke presents two stories about Philip (his interaction with Simon the magician and the Ethiopian eunuch). But then Saul's story picks up again in Acts 9, with the notice that he wished to expand his persecution of the church from Jerusalem to Damascus. Two events are central to the story: Saul's encounter with Jesus on the road to Damascus and the call for Ananias to seek out Saul.

Structure. The lectionary reading offers two different boundaries, vv. 1-6 and 7-20. The following outline and commentary will follow the larger boundary. Acts 9:1-20 separates into two parts: the theophany of Jesus on the Damascus road, which causes blindness to Saul (vv. 1-9); and the call of Ananias to lift Saul's blindness and to baptize him, along with a closing notice of Saul preaching (vv. 10-20).

Significance. Acts 9 is about Saul's conversion. The conversion is described through the motif of "the way" (Greek, *hodos*). This term is used in v. 2 to describe Christians when Saul asks the high priest

111

for "letters to the synagogues of Damascus so that if he found any who belonged to the Way (Greek, *hodou*), men or women, he might bring them bound to Jerusalem." The implied meaning of "the Way" in this verse is most certainly "the way of Jesus." The narrative makes it clear that Saul's aim is to persecute the people of "the Way," which is described later in v. 17 by Ananias as Saul's "way." The Greek of v. 17 literally reads, "the Lord Jesus who appeared to you in the way [*hodoi*] in which you were going." Note the inadequacy of the NRSV translation, "The Lord Jesus, who appeared to you on your way here." The framing of the story with the motif of the way underscores how Saul's conversion is a change from following his own life's course aimed at persecuting to a new course of following Jesus, which will require tutoring in what it means to suffer instead of persecute (v. 16). Luke has constructed a rich tapestry to describe how Saul changed his way, yet he is not really the hero of the story. That role is reserved for Ananias.

Verses 1-9 describe a theophany that leads to blindness. Luke uses many classical motifs that often accompany theophanies. The appearance of God as light is customary, but the point of emphasis is on speech rather than sight. Note how the flash of light gives way to a conversation between Jesus and Saul, and how it is emphasized that Saul's companions heard a voice but saw nothing. No one on the road to Damascus sees Jesus and this seems to be the point of the text. Theophany is not conversion. It is simply a confrontation that confirms blindness.

Verses 10-20 are structured as a call narrative, but the call is to Ananias and not Saul. See the commentary for Year A, Proper 17 for discussion of call narratives. The setting and introductory word to Ananias are sketched out in v. 10, which leads to a commission in vv. 11-12. Ananias is told to seek out Saul and lay his hands on him so that he might regain his sight. Ananias objects in vv. 13-14 by providing a character reference of Saul as someone who has inflicted great evil on Christians in Jerusalem. God provides reassurance to Ananias in vv. 15-16 that God has chosen Saul for a mission, and that God will personally tutor Saul in the meaning of suffering. In vv. 17-20 Ananias responds to God's call, which moves Saul from blindness to sight, prompting his baptism. The story ends with Saul now firmly anchored in the way of Jesus and proclaiming the gospel in the synagogue.

Two themes can be explored in preaching this text. The first is the contrast between the way of Jesus and the way of Saul as a contrast between suffering for God (v. 16) and persecuting others for God (vv. 4-5). The second theme is conversion. Saul's conversion is frequently associated with his experience of theophany on the road to Damascus in vv. 1-9. This event certainly stopped him in his tracks, but it is not his conversion. It is an experience that simply confirmed his blindness. If conversion is the focal point, then the real hero of the story is Ananias in vv. 10-20. He is the one who goes through the standard call form in order to seek out his enemy, whom, upon seeing, he addresses as brother. Luke has structured the conversion of Saul in such a way that despite all the fireworks, the story could not reach its conclusion without the disciple Ananias answering a less flashy and somewhat risky call from God to seek out the blind Saul. It is his action that brings sight to Saul. When this story is examined in its larger context, then it becomes clear that Ananias parallels the role of Philip in the previous two stories of Acts 8, while Saul becomes another example of how the way of Jesus was spreading like wildfire.

The Response: *Psalm 30*

A Hymn of Thanksgiving

Setting. Psalm 30 is a hymn of thanksgiving over having been healed. Verse 2 reads: "O LORD my God, I cried to you for help, and you have healed me."

Structure. Psalm 30 separates into three parts. It begins in vv. 1-3 with praise to God for rescuing the psalmist. Verses 4-5 shift the focus from God to fellow worshipers when the psalmist calls for those around him to join in giving thanksgiving to God. In vv. 6-12 the psalmist recounts his life changes and how God rescued him. This section closes with a summary statement outlining the purpose of divine deliverance: It is so that the psalmist can continue to praise God.

Significance. The central motif of healing does not provide a direct response to the story of Saul's conversion. Yet central to the account of divine healing is the emphasis on a change of direction that was experienced by the psalmist. He recounts his movement from prosperity (v. 6) to near death (v. 9) and back again to the world of the living (v. 11). This emphasis on direction provides a point of contact to the motif of the Way in Acts 9 and how Saul's conversion is characterized as a change of direction. Once this point of contact is made, the language of the psalm, with its emphasis on sickness and divine healing, then provides commentary on Saul, especially with his movement from persecutor with a clear focus to being blind, which finally results in sight.

New Testament Texts

Both passages for this Sunday present scenes concerned with the resurrected Jesus Christ. The reading from Revelation tells of events in heaven, whereas the Gospel lesson recounts a post-resurrection appearance of Jesus to the disciples in Galilee. Revelation portrays heavenly worship and invites us to experience the praise of our Savior. John's story is primarily a commissioning scene, directing disciples of Jesus into mission.

The Epistle: *Revelation 5:11-14*

Celebrating the Worth of the Lamb

Setting. Following the letters to the seven congregations in Asia Minor in Revelation 2–3 we come in Revelation 4 to the account of the first great heavenly vision reported by John (4:1–11:19). This vision has many distinct scenes. Generally Revelation 4 reports the activities of the heavenly community at worship, and the primary focus is God on the throne. Then, in chapter 5 John of Patmos begins to shift the focus to "the Lamb" who alone is said to be worthy to open the scroll held by God on the throne. This shift signals the beginning of a refocusing from heaven at worship to heaven at work. The refocusing is complete at the outset of Revelation 6.

We deal here with highly dramatic apocalyptic material wherein the symbolism is rich, intriguing, and difficult. We must come to this text recognizing initially that it speaks of the Kingship or Lordship of God (throne), the significance and accomplishments of Christ's saving death (Lamb, worthy), and the unfolding of God's will in relation to the course of cosmic events (the scroll contains the effective statements of God's will).

Structure. Revelation 5:1-14 is a complex, but coherent, dramatic scene. The account is narrated through parataxis ("And . . . and . . . and. . . ."). The major moments in the account are introduced with the phrase "and I saw" in Greek (5:1, 2, 6, 11—also 6:1), so that our text, 5:11-14, is a distinct portion of the report of the vision. Even this "scene" has distinguishable elements:

(1) the voices of the 10,000 times 10,000 angels utter a doxology to the Lamb (vv. 11-12);

(2) all creatures in the cosmos praise God and Christ (v. 13); and

(3) the reactions of the four living creatures and the elders provide a finale to the worship (v. 14)

Significance. The chorus of 100,000,000 angels—numbered in a manner reminiscent of Daniel 7:10—offers magnificent praise to the Lamb. The words of the doxology in v. 12*b* echo and expand the praise uttered earlier in this scene at 5:9-10, and indeed, that earlier praise itself took up language from the opening thanksgiving to the book of Revelation (1:5*b*-6—see the comments on last Sunday's text from Revelation). In the time following Easter the angels' praise reminds us of the unsurpassable significance of the saving death (and resurrection) of Jesus Christ without attempting to give a mechanical explanation of the operation of salvation. Thus, the text does not point in the direction of a didactic sermon. Rather, the praise is pure confession, not the delineation of historical cause-and-effect.

Yet, the language of the doxology is noteworthy. First, the title "Lamb" is the most frequent designation for Jesus in the book of Revelation. The meaning of this title in Revelation is similar to the use of the word as a title in other New Testament writings, most notably the gospel according to John (for example, 1:29) and I Corinthians 5:7. The title "Lamb" plays off the image of the Passover lamb, the blood of which marked out the children of Israel for life as God rescued them from bondage in Egypt; and in subsequent developments in Jewish reflection on the lamb, the blood of the Paschal lamb was believed to have atoning effects for the sins of Israel. Second, seven assertions are made concerning the Lamb. Commentators point out that the first four items are typical properties of God's divine character, whereas the last three elements are outright praise. Thus, inherent in this lofty praise is a theology of divine atonement for human sin in and through the death (and resurrection) of Jesus Christ. The old gospel song, "Are You Washed in the Blood of the Lamb" would not have completely offended John of Patmos.

In v. 13 the praise of Christ moves past the boundaries of heaven to encompass all the cosmos. The threefold division of creation here is similar to the phrases of Paul's hymnic passage of praise in Philippians 2:10. The vision here is of cosmic hegemony—that is, the ranks (divisions!) of created order are now united in the mutual praise of Christ. Thus, we see the goal of the Lamb's self-sacrifice— namely, the establishment of harmony in a broken and sinful world. God the Creator works in and through Jesus Christ the Redeemer, so that we see the Creator and Redeemer are one as through the divine work of Christ creation is itself united.

Finally, in v. 14 the four creatures and the elders deliver the liturgical conclusion to the praise of the Lamb. The "Amen!" (a liturgical cry meaning "let it be so!") and the humble posture of the elders epitomize the essence of true worship. Thus, in the context of Easter this text invites us to join in the celebration of the death and resurrection of Jesus Christ. We are told that heaven itself sets the precedent for our worship, and in a subtle manner this scene informs us that in the death and resurrection of Christ we see the person, power, and glory of God.

The Gospel: *John 21:1-19*

When the Lord's Disciples Went Fishing

Setting. This lesson follows immediately on the verses of last week's Gospel lesson. Readers may consult the previous discussion of setting for a general orientation to the literary position of this week's lesson. One should notice above all that this Sunday's text follows 20:30-31. Thus, we come to an epilogue to the Gospel according to John with the verses of our lesson. Moreover, the ambiguous beginning of 21:1, "After this . . . ," leaves the question of the time or date of this account completely open, so that in a sense we encounter a "timeless" narrative.

Structure. At least three lines of early Christian tradition are united in the verses of our lesson—a post-resurrection appearance story, a meal-scene with strong eucharistic overtones, and a commissioning scene—and as is clear from v. 14 there are at least two distinct units of material. Comparison of this account with a strikingly similar story set in Luke 5:1-11 in the context of Jesus' pre-Passion ministry suggests that the lines of tradition behind our lesson may be even more complex than we can imagine. Nevertheless, we find here an intricately woven tapestry of traditions that directs our reflection as we follow its delicate presentation.

As we move through the narrative we find the following themes: the post-Easter presence of Jesus among the disciples; the joy of recognizing the resurrected Lord; the Lord's bountiful provision for his disciples; the "real presence" of the Lord "at table" with the disciples; and the Lord's direction of devotion into action. One or all of these themes are appropriate topics for preaching in the Easter season.

Significance. We find Peter and the other disciples named in this story in Galilee fishing. Having followed Jesus in the course of his ministry, having gone with him to Jerusalem, having known or seen him crucified, having encountered him raised from the dead, and having received from him the Holy Spirit—what do the disciples do? They go fishing. They return to doing what they were doing before Christ came into their lives. As we meet the group here, discipleship does not seem to mean a call to ministry. Having gotten the Holy Spirit, it does not appear that the Holy Spirit got them!

Yet, we see that as the disciples return to the normal patterns of human existence, the risen Jesus Christ seeks them out once again. Whether or not we should understand that the disciples have come to take the risen Jesus for granted, the story informs us that he did not abandon them. He came to them as they fished, there in the middle of their everyday lives, and he blessed them in a way that was both unexpected and seemingly more than anything for which they could have hoped.

117

In and through the blessing at least one disciple recognized the presence of the Lord. His recognition prompted the impetuous act of Peter, who having led the others on this fishing outing now abandoned them for the overwhelming joy of the presence of the Lord. Good friends and many fishes were left behind for the company of the risen Lord.

When the disciples made it to shore they encountered even more of the Lord's bountiful provision. He came to them, filling their nets with fishes and their hearts with joy; and now, they find that he offers them breakfast. In the offer of food, however, we should see the first hint of the intention of the risen Christ to direct his disciples to mission. "Bring some of the fish you caught . . . come and have breakfast." Called to the Lord's meal, the disciples are directed to bring something (given to them by the Lord) into the feast. What the disciples experienced on the shore is what every Lord's Supper should be for the Church today: The Lord's people called to the Lord's Table, bringing something of the Lord's provision, and eating in the mysterious assurance of the real presence of the Lord. The story tells us it was almost too much for the disciples, who in their wonder still "knew" it was the Lord.

The story continues by telling of the conversation between Jesus and Simon Peter. Commentators often observe that the threefold questioning and the threefold direction are a dramatic "un-doing" of the earlier threefold denial of Christ by Peter. Whether or not we may make that equation, we should see that it is the risen Lord who calls Peter's love and devotion into action. Simply loving the Lord—that is, merely feeling good about Jesus—is not the stuff of true discipleship. Disciples who love the Lord put the strength of their devotion into concrete action as they give themselves in service to the humans for whom Christ himself lived, died, and is raised.

Easter 3: The Celebration

If today's service emphasizes either the eucharistic portion of the Easter Vigil by dividing it up among the early Sundays of Easter as discussed on pp. 88-89 or if the emphasis is on Jesus' meal with the disciples in the Gospel reading, the following opening prayer is recommended:

> O God, whose blessed Son made himself known to his disciples in the breaking of bread: Open the eyes of our faith, that we may behold him in all his redeeming work; who lives and reigns with you, in the unity of the Holy Spirit, one God, now and for ever. (*Book of Common Prayer*, pp. 224-25)

The petition for the opening of our eyes also recalls Saul's experience in the house of Ananias in the reading from Acts.

Anglican and Roman Catholic churches celebrate January 25 as the Feast of the Conversion of St. Paul in its own right. If the preacher makes that the emphasis today, the Episcopal collect for January 25 would be a fitting opening prayer:

> O God, by the preaching of your apostle Paul you have caused the light of the Gospel to shine throughout the world: Grant, we pray, that we, having his wonderful conversion in remembrance, may show ourselves thankful to you by following his holy teaching; through Jesus Christ our Lord. (*Book of Common Prayer*, pp. 238-39)

Because Peter and Paul both figure prominently in today's readings, the following collect would also be appropriate:

> Almighty God, whose blessed apostles Peter and Paul glorified you in life and in death: Grant that your Church, instructed by their teaching and example, and knit together by your Spirit, may ever stand firm upon the one foundation, which is Jesus Christ our Lord; who lives and reigns with you, in the unity of the Holy Spirit, one God, now and for ever. (*Book of Common Prayer*, p. 241, adapted)

This collect might also be used in the intercessions when prayers are asked for the unity of the Church.

A little-known hymn text around the theme of the conversion of St. Paul is "We Sing the Glorious Conquest" in the Episcopal *Hymnal 1982*, no. 255. It is set there to the familiar tune Munich.

The meal of fish in the Gospel reading has eucharistic overtones because in the early Church the fish (I X TH U S = Jesus Christ, God's Son, Savior) was a symbol for Christ. Here we see Christ as the host at the meal in which he gives himself. Fish and different forms of the IXTHUS symbol could be prominently displayed in the visuals for today.

Fourth Sunday of Easter

Old Testament Texts

Acts 9:36-43 is a miracle story in which Peter raises Tabitha from the dead. Psalm 23 is a song of confidence in spite of danger and death.

The Lesson: *Acts 9:36-43*

Peter Raises Tabitha from the Dead

Setting. Acts 9:36-43 is the second of two miracle stories about Peter. The first miracle is described in Acts 9:32-35, when Peter heals the paralyzed Aeneas. The second is the lectionary text for this Sunday, the raising of Tabitha from the dead. These two stories follow loosely a stereotyped pattern in which the scene of the miracle is established (Lydda for the first miracle and Joppa for the second); followed by an exposition of the illness (Aeneas is paralyzed, and Tabitha is dead); then an act of healing which includes both a word and a gesture ("Aeneas, Jesus Christ heals you; get up and make your bed." "Tabitha, get up."); some kind of result or demonstration of the miracle; and finally a conclusion showing how the miracle affected the believers ("And all the residents of Lydda and Sharon saw him and turned to the Lord." "This became known throughout Joppa, and many believed in the Lord").

Structure. The lectionary text includes only the second miracle story in Acts 9:36-43. One may wish to expand the reading to include both miracle stories, but then a decision must be made as to whether v. 31 should also be included to provide an overall introduction to this section, when it is noted that the church throughout

120

Samaria, Judea, and Galilee has peace, and that it was thriving in the power of the Holy Spirit.

Significance. What is the point of inserting two miracle stories at the end of Acts 9? The larger context of Acts provides an important starting point for answering this question. Luke has been sketching the growth of the early church through a sequence of stories in chapters 8–9. There were two stories of Philip bringing the gospel to Simon the magician and the Ethiopian eunuch (Acts 8:4-40), and then the account of Saul's conversion (Acts 9:1-30). Acts 9:31 summarizes this section by noting how the church was growing throughout Judea, Galilee, and Samaria. With the conversion of Saul and the saturation of the church throughout Palestine, the reader is now prepared for the next major move in the story of the early church, which is the mission to the Gentiles. But it is Peter and not Paul who will take center stage in this transition. The two miracle stories of Peter in Acts 9:32-35 and 36-43 on the one hand provide an interlude to the conversion of Cornelius in Acts 10, while, on the other hand, the raising of Tabitha actually foreshadows the events that are about to take place through its inner biblical interpretation of Elijah in I Kings 17:17-24.

Although miracle stories are common in the ministry of Jesus, they are rare in the Old Testament. Only twice does a prophet raise someone from the dead. Once Elijah raises the son of the widow of Zarephath from the dead (I Kings 17:17-24), and another time Elisha resuscitates the Shunammite's son (II Kings 4:8-37). A comparison suggests that Luke has loosely modeled Peter's miracle of the raising of Tabitha from the dead on the miracle story of Elijah raising the son of the widow of Zarephath from the dead. The points of contact not only include the similar miracle (raising someone from the dead), but also the similar setting (an upper room), and a similar response (belief). Once the inner biblical interpretation between Elijah in I Kings 17:17-24 and Peter in Acts 9:36-43 is noted, then the reason for it also becomes clear. Zarephath was a town in Sidon, where Elijah was forced to flee because of his conflict with Ahab. Thus, his miracle was performed on a Gentile. By constructing the miracle of Peter as an inner biblical interpretation of Elijah in Sidon, Luke has prepared the reader for the mission to the Gentiles. Fur-

121

thermore, the ethnicity of Tabitha (alias Dorcas) is not clear from the story in Acts 9:36-43, and perhaps this too is intentional, since the important piece of information is not her genealogy, but that she was a disciple, who "was full of good work and acts of charity" (v. 36).

The Response: *Psalm 23*

The Lord Is My Shepherd

Setting. Psalm 23 is one of the most familiar psalms in scripture. We all learn it as children and over time the pastoral imagery of God as our shepherd becomes almost romantic. This is unfortunate, because even though Psalm 23 is about security, it is not a romantic psalm. In fact the background of the psalm is just the reverse. Danger is looming large for the singer of this prayer song. Verse 4 provides the setting, and it includes images of death and evil. The confession of God's security as a shepherd must be seen against this background.

Structure. The psalm could be separated into three parts: vv. 1-2, a confession of God as shepherd; vv. 3-4, a description of the wanderer; and vv. 5-6 a description of God as host. Verses 3-4, however, are not necessarily a description of wandering as much as they are a description of threat. A two-part division might better convey the message of the psalm: vv. 1-4, a confession of God as shepherd in the context of threat; and vv. 5-6, a confession of divine security in the context of the worshiping community.

Significance. The significance of Psalm 23 is in the contrast between the two parts, which underscore the security of God as a shepherd. The first section of the psalm divides between a description of God as shepherd in vv. 1-3 and the situation of the psalmist in v. 4. God is a shepherd, who is able to lead, restore, and provide nurture (vv. 1-3), even in the darkest situations (v. 4), because he is never absent from us. Note the only direct address to God in vv. 1-4 occurs in v. 4 ("For you are with me."). This confession underscores how God is present even when we have moved to the outer reaches of God's domain and thus come under the shadow of death. The scene changes abruptly, however, in vv. 5-6 from threat and death to a banquet as the worshiper moves into the very presence of God within the sanctuary. Here the metaphors for God shift from shepherd in a threatening situation to host within the security of a home. God prepares a banquet for worshiper and enemies. This shift in imagery from shepherd to host underscores how worship is where our real security lies. As one commentator on this psalm states, worship is the sphere where God's protection is most readily available. This reality is underscored through the motif of anointing in v. 5, which gives rise to a whole new perspective on the part of the worshiper. The threat of enemies in pursuit through a valley of death shifts in v. 6 to the pursuit of goodness and mercy in the temple of God—even while the enemies look on. The confession of the worshiper in v. 6 is anything but a romantic vision, for it goes against our notions of security.

New Testament Texts

The reading from Revelation presents material in the context of the opening of the seven seals of the scroll of God. The message of this end-time vision is that our experience is not always a reliable tool for the evaluation of ultimate truth, because it does not contain the final word on either God's character or the content of God's salvation. The lesson from John takes up the issue of Jesus' identity and makes it clear that God grants the gift of recognition.

The Epistle: *Revelation 7:9-17*

Red Makes White

Setting. Last week we considered the general setting in which this reading occurs—namely, the first great vision scene in Revelation 4:1–11:19. More specifically, Revelation 7:9-17 comes in the context of the opening of the seven seals (Revelation 6:1–8:5), which describes eschatological catastrophes that will accompany the close of this age. Revelation 7 is often described as an interlude between the sixth (Revelation 6:12-17) and seventh (Revelation 8:1-5) seals. The chapter presents a description of the Church being persecuted at the close of the present age (vv. 1-8) and a picture of the Church in heaven in the new age after the saints have passed through the period of persecution (vv. 9-17). These portraits of the Church have been contrasted by past interpreters as the Church militant in the present age and the Church triumphant in the age to come. The lectionary lesson for this Sunday is the latter half of chapter 7, the picture of the Church triumphant in the age to come, but it cannot be interpreted without an understanding of what it means for the Church to be militant.

Structure. The picture of the Church triumphant separates into a heavenly vision in vv. 9-12 and the interpretation of this vision to John in vv. 13-17. The text can be outlined in the following manner.

I. The Heavenly Vision of John (vv. 9-12)
    A. The song of the great multitude (vv. 9-10)
        1. Setting (v. 9)
        2. Speech (v. 10)
    B. The Song of the Angels (vv. 11-12)
        1. Setting (v. 11)
        2. Speech (v. 12)
II. The Interpretation of the Heavenly Vision (vv. 13-17)
    A. The elder's question (v. 13)
    B. John's response (v. 14)
    C. The elder's answer (vv. 14-17)
        1. Identification of the church during persecution in this age (v. 14)
        2. Identification of the church after persecution in the age to come (vv. 15-17)

The heavenly vision in vv. 9-12 separates into two songs by two different groups. First, all the saints from every nation are described as singing before the throne of the lamb with two symbols of victory (white robes and palm branches). The song in v. 10 is not about their salvation, but about the greatness of God who is able to save. Second, the angels pick up the song of praise from v. 10 and expand it with a seven-fold ascription of praise in v. 12. The scene shifts from heaven to earth (and presumably from the future to the present) in v. 13-17 with the exchange between the elder and John. The elder provides the identification of the white-robed singers in two time

frames. At the close of the age they were the ones who were persecuted (v. 14), and they now live in the eschatological age (vv. 15-
17). The imagery for both parts of this interpretation comes from
Isaiah. The imagery of red blood turning white is addressed in Isaiah
1:18 and the eschatological vision is from Isaiah 49:10.

Significance. The larger context of the seven seals as signifiers of
tribulations must be kept clearly in mind when interpreting Revelation 7:9-17, for it underscores how the snapshot of the eschatological
age is being taken during a time of persecution. Thus the present
experience of the Church at the time of John's writing does not support in any way his future vision of it. More than one leader in modern apocalyptic communities have failed to recognize this discontinuity, including Vernon Howell (alias David Koresh) in Waco, Texas,
when at least 80 of his followers were led to their fiery deaths at the
time of this writing. The power of this text lies precisely in this discontinuity, for it states that our experience in this world cannot be a
reliable indicator of the character of God or even of the quality of our
salvation. John makes this point through the central image of the text
in v. 14, when the elder, who is interpreting the vision to John, makes
the paradoxical statement that the robes of the saints have been made
white by washing them in red blood. This is an illogical statement
because no amount of experience will support such a conclusion. Red
doesn't make white. In the same way persecution to the point of
death cannot be redefined as victory on the basis of the experience
itself. Persecution is persecution. And death is death. The point and
the power of the end-time vision is that it underscores how experience is not always reliable, because it does not contain the final word
on either God's character or the content of his salvation. God can
make a robe white by washing it in red. This story is in many ways a
critique of our everyday experience because in pondering it we share
in John's end-time vision as told in Revelation 7:9-17.

The Gospel: *John 10:22-30*

God's Granting of Jesus' Sheep

Setting. The lectionary includes the majority of John 10:1-30 in
the Gospel lessons by dividing the verses into three units (vv. 1-10,

125

11-18, 22-30) and respectively presenting them on the Fourth Sunday of Easter in Years A, B, and C. The material in 10:1-18 actually follows closely on the incident of the healing of the man born blind in John 9:1-41 by offering a christological meditation on the theme "Christ the Good Shepherd." As the omission of vv. 19-21 of John 10 from the lectionary indicates, there is a clear break between the material in the first half of John 10 and the material that follows, beginning with our lesson. Nevertheless, the mention of sheep in vv. 26-27 suggests a loose relationship between the parts of the larger chapter, so that a reading of the whole of John 10 may help orient the mind for preaching the verses of the lesson.

The temporal setting for our lesson is provided by v. 22—it is winter, at the festival of the Dedication of the Temple, that is, Hanukkah. Thus, in an indirect manner the time indicates a contrast between pride and confidence in the Temple on the one hand and refusal to have faith in Jesus on the other. That John intends the contrast seems clear from the statement that God "sanctified"—that is, "consecrated" or "dedicated"—Jesus and sent him into the world in 10:36.

Structure. The verses of the lesson are a brief, unified account that finds a complementary conclusion in vv. 31-39. The narrative unfolds as (1) Jesus' presence provokes (2) a question about his messianic identity that, in turn, solicits (3) his confronting the questioners with their refusal to believe in him and, then, he continues (4) by speaking of the relationship between him and his "sheep," (5) the role "the Father" plays in his work, and (6) the unity between the Father and him. Provocative presence, question, confrontation, and revelatory declarations make up the substance of this story—the whole account focuses on Jesus and, ultimately, on God.

Significance. Interpreters have long suggested that in the history of early Christian tradition there is some relationship between the exchange reported here and that recorded in Luke 22:67-68 (69?), so that at its heart this lesson is about the rigid refusal of certain of Jesus' Jewish contemporaries, especially the leaders in Jerusalem, to recognize who he was and what were his purposes. The language of the passage is typical of the Gospel according to John: Jesus speaks in symbols and metaphors, often confrontationally, but frequently with the ultimate purpose of making revelatory declarations; moreover, the opponents of Jesus are referred to as "the Jews" (in the time of the story Jesus and his "sheep" are also Jews!), a designation that shows that the older Jesus traditions had life in the later historical setting of hostility between church and synagogue. Thus we see that despite the straightforward appearance of our lesson, the verses are remarkably complex and invite if not require careful study and sophisticated interpretation.

In the lines preceding our lesson, Jesus had spoken of himself as the gate for the sheep and as the Good Shepherd who lays down his life for the sheep—metaphors referring to Jesus Christ as the way to salvation and to Jesus' death as a voluntary act in compliance with God's will for the achievement of salvation. Even on the surface without the rich theological interpretation, the language about sheep and shepherd makes sense as a background to Jesus' adversaries' question, for the shepherd was a well-known symbol in Judaism for the long-awaited Davidic king. John tells us in his own way that the very words of Jesus called forth the questions about his possible messianic identity.

When the question was asked, however, Jesus was neither purely polite nor sheerly straightforward with his answer. Rather, Jesus confronts his examiners with their refusal to see the plain evidence that God lays before them in the work that Jesus did in God's name. Yet, the problem is not merely their will not to believe, for they are not Jesus' sheep—so they cannot believe! God gives Jesus the sheep of his fold, the sheep do not self-generate. Yet, ultimately this statement about relationships is interpreted to point to the oneness of Jesus and his Father, a bold theological statement about Christ's divinity, but also a statement about how humans know God.

The ideas expressed in this passage raise difficult questions, and it is necessary to ponder these lines in context. First, God is portrayed here as being in control of the constitution of Jesus' flock. Our lesson expresses a bold confidence in God despite the reality of opposition—initially to Jesus, then to the Church. Moreover, we find that the eyes of faith see more in the person and work of Jesus than merely the man from Nazareth. Second, we learn something about human nature in our lesson. Whatever we have and whoever we are is the result of God's relating to us. Even the eyes of faith that see are God's good provision. Third, the will to present the polemical logic of this lesson came out of a first-century situation of real hostility between Christians, often former Jews, and the members of the synagogue who were dubious of Christian christological claims. Ancient intramural rivalry gave force to lines like these, and such passages often provided comfort for Christians who felt themselves persecuted. Today we should lay aside the polemical dimension of this lesson, but in doing so we recognize that it is not necessary to discount the theology and the Christology of the text. Rather, we seek to speak of God and Christ with relevance and energy in a new day.

Easter 4: The Celebration

The readings from John 10 and the use of Psalm 23 on the Fourth Sunday of Easter in all three years of the lectionary cycle underscore its popular designation as "Good Shepherd Sunday." This becomes the controlling image and should inform the use of visuals on this day. A large number of representations of the Good Shepherd from the ancient world to the present day might be displayed around the church.

The Book of Common Prayer incorporates the shepherd image in its opening prayer for the day:

> O God, whose Son Jesus is the good shepherd of your people:
> Grant that when we hear his voice we may know him who
> calls us each by name, and follow where he leads; who, with
> you and the Holy Spirit, lives and reigns, one God, for ever
> and ever. (p. 225)

The Acts lesson should be used in preaching today as illustrative of what it means to be a part of that community which has Jesus as the Good Shepherd. The lesson from Revelation projects our confidence in the Shepherd into all eternity. It is John who provides four verbs to describe the relationship between sheep and Shepherd. The sheep hear and follow; the Shepherd knows and gives eternal life. The raising of Tabitha is a sign of that eternal life given by Christ, and John's vision provides assurance of Christ's everlasting care. The preacher may wish to structure a sermon around the dynamic involved between the four verbs.

The preacher may also wish to approach the sermon by way of the paradox in Revelation 7:17, the Lamb becomes the shepherd. This can provide an opportunity to examine the strange reversals that are occasioned by lives of faithful discipleship.

Most hymnals will contain at least one metrical paraphrase of Psalm 23 that can be sung as the psalm for the day.

Fifth Sunday of Easter

Old Testament Texts

Acts 11:1-18 narrates Peter's report to the Jerusalem church concerning the conversion of Cornelius. Psalm 148 is a hymn of praise.

The Lesson: *Acts 11:1-18*

The Gospel Is for All

Setting. The events surrounding the conversion of Cornelius in Acts 10:1–11:18 are pivotal to the book of Acts, because it underscores the central problem that faced the early church in their attempt to interpret the gospel. The issue simply put is this: Is the good news for all people? And if so, what are the implications for proclaiming the gospel? Or, to state the problem in contemporary language: How must the gospel be contextualized?

Luke considered the challenge of contextualizing the gospel to be so important for the early church that the only other story in the book of Acts to receive as much attention as the conversion of Cornelius is the account of Pentecost in Acts 2. In fact, some scholars suggest that the conversion of Cornelius is best interpreted as yet another Pentecost, "when the gift of the Holy Spirit had been poured out even on the Gentiles" (Acts 10:45).

Structure. Three problems in structure must be noted. First, Peter's report to the Jerusalem church consists mainly of a repetition of the events that happened to him in Acts 10. Thus the entire section of Acts 10:1–11:18 must be kept in mind when preaching Acts 11:1-18. Second, Acts 11:1-18 does not make clear the tension and resistance that is central to this story with regard to Peter. His report to the Jerusalem church concerning the conversion of Cornelius is in many ways also a report about his own conversion. Verse 17 reads, "If then God gave them the same gift that he gave us when we believed in the Lord Jesus Christ, who was I that I could hinder God?" Third, as noted above, the outpouring of the Holy Spirit that is reported by Peter in Acts 11:17 must be read in conjunction with Pentecost in Acts 2. This relationship will provide our point of entry for interpreting the conversion of Cornelius.

Significance. The book of Acts begins with the outpouring of the Holy Spirit on the disciples. This marks the inauguration of the Church, and Peter takes on a central role in the event, especially with his sermon (see Acts 2:14-40). Although the seeds of a universal mission are planted in this sermon (Acts 2:9-11, 39), the primary focus is Israel (Acts 2:14, 22, 36). The focus on Israel is maintained throughout the early chapters of Acts so that the gospel first takes root in the larger context of Judaism, which is only natural, because the disciples themselves are religious Jews. The result of this is that the gospel was first interpreted within the larger context of Judaism—hence the early church was kosher and law-observing. The conversion of Cornelius is a central story in Acts because it is being used by Luke to force the early church to come to grips with the limitations of their own ethnicity and cultural context in proclaiming a universal gospel.

Peter plays a primary role in this second Pentecost story, just as he did in the first, but he is not the central character in Acts 10:1–11:18. Notice how Acts 10 begins with Cornelius, who is presented as one who seeks God independently, and how an angel of God directs him to Peter. (This is very similar to the relationship of the Ethiopian eunuch and Philip.) The challenge for Peter, when he enters the story, is whether he can recognize the work of God when it does not conform to the cultural context in which he appropriated the gospel. This is no easy matter, and Peter initially fails by not understanding the vision of clean and unclean food. Yet, once Peter is properly instructed by Cornelius, he acquires insight and concludes: "I truly understand that God shows no partiality, but in every nation anyone who fears him and does what is right is acceptable to him" (10:35-36). Peter's ability to see God's salvation even when it did not conform to his own cultural context is so significant that it prompts a second Pentecost even before he could finish speaking (10:44). This insight is the cornerstone of his report to the Jerusalem church in Acts 11:1-18, when, after seeing the gift of the Holy Spirit being given to Cornelius, Peter asks the rhetorical question of the leaders in v. 17, "who was I that I should hinder God?"

If we simply read the account of the conversion of Cornelius in the historical past, then it becomes easy to see the problem, first, of Peter, and, then, of the Jerusalem church, which later criticized Peter for eating with uncircumcised people (11:2). How could the Jerusalem church elevate kosher laws to such a degree where these laws became a prerequisite for presenting the gospel to all people? The challenge of peaching this text is to communicate that the conversion of Cornelius is not a story about the irrelevance of kosher laws. Rather it is a story about the importance of contextualizing the gospel, and the need for Christians to see the saving activity of God in cultural contexts, which are unfamiliar to us. The problem of contextualizing the gospel is multifaceted. It is not a call to deny our own cultural context for interpreting the gospel, but to recognize and to encourage the work of the Spirit in people who are different. A sermon on this text could explore this problem at the level of distinct national and international cultures, but the preacher might also probe the "culture" of a specific congregation. What are its kosher laws? If a local congregation can meet the challenge of contextualizing the gospel, then Luke would say that they, along with Peter, have experienced yet another Pentecost.

The Response: *Psalm 148*

A Hymn of Praise

Setting. Psalm 148 is probably best categorized as a hymn of praise in which imperatival forms of the verb predominate (note the repetition of the imperative, Praise! or Let them praise! in vv. 1, 2, 3, 4, 5, 7, 13, 14). The scope of the psalm is so wide in its call to praise that all aspects of creation are included. This larger vision gives rise to a second characteristic of this hymn, which is the strong presence of wisdom motifs, especially evident in the list of the natural order as those called upon to praise God.

Structure. The psalm separates into two parts, vv. 1-6 and 7-14. Verses 1-6 are a call to praise God from heaven, while vv. 7-14 repeat the command but this time from the earth. Each of these sections further separates into three parts: (1) Each section begins with a command to praise (from heaven, vv. 1-4 and from earth, vv. 7-12). (2) The command is followed in each case with a summary statement, which includes a reason why God should be praised (vv. 5 and 13). This section is signaled in each case through the repetition of the phrase, Let them praise the name of the Lord (vv. 5*a* and 13*a*). The reason for praise from the hosts of heaven is that God created them (v. 5*b*), while earthly creatures must praise God because only the Lord is exalted on earth (v. 13*b*)! (3) Finally, each section ends with a summary statement about God (vv. 6 and 14) in relationship to the hosts of heaven and earth (specifically Israel).

Significance. The universal dimension of the call to praise provides a fitting response to the conversion of Cornelius the Gentile in Acts 10:1–11:18. One of the points of the psalm is that no one voice is sufficient to carry the praise of God. Thus, the psalm calls for all voices throughout creation (vv. 1-6) and from all nations (7-14) to join in a single symphony of praise to God. Acts 11:1-18 lacks the creation imagery of Psalm 148:1-6, but its closing verse, in which the Jerusalem church is described as follows, "And they praised God, saying, Then God has given even to the Gentiles the repentance that leads to life" (v. 18), certainly picks up the melody of vv. 7-14.

New Testament Texts

These lessons are about two crucial themes of Christian faith. Both, however, are concerned with the transforming power of God that brings new life and the glory of God's future. Thus, though they are different in tone, both texts are powerful declarations of good news. The reading from Revelation is intensely concerned with the future, although as a message about the ultimate revelation and accomplishments of God's glory at the end they are certainly meant to inspire hope for life before the end. The lesson from John presents Jesus' "new commandment" to his disciples—that is, the commandment to love one another (in the same selfless fashion that he loved them) in order that the world around them, not yet part of the community of light, might recognize in them the truth and the glory of God's own love (manifested in the first place in Jesus Christ).

The Epistle: *Revelation 21:1-6*

Seeing the End and Knowing What It Means

Setting. General introductory remarks to the book of Revelation were offered in relation to the readings for the Second Sunday of Easter; readers may turn there for that information. Again, on this Sunday we should recall, however, that recognizing the particular literary style in which a section is written assists greatly in interpreting the text.

The general segment of the book from which our lesson comes is a great vision of the end that is recorded in 19:1–22:5. More specifically, our text is part of the vision of the new Jerusalem and the final word of God, 21:1-8. This is the final vision in a series of visions reported throughout the larger section.

Structure. These six verses are loaded! First, John of Patmos, the seer of Revelation, beholds the new heaven and the new earth. Second, he observes the descent of the new Jerusalem. Third, as John watches, a voice from the throne interprets the twin-vision by declaring the nature of the new relationship established between God and humans at the end. And, fourth, "the one who was seated on the throne" gives John a command to write, and then, (fifth?) that same figure (God) declares the completion of the divine work of redemption.

Significance. The vision is actually a double vision, telling of the same divine work in two ways (vv. 1-2). The voice explains the meaning of the events (vv. 3-4), and the truth of the vision and the explanation is confirmed by God himself (vv. 5-6).

The reporting of a vision is typical of apocalyptic literature, though as we can see, a prophetic declaration is reported in the course of John's telling of the vision. As ideas develop, apocalyptic literature is kin to prophetic literature, but it seems to come from a situation of persecution and to be directed to people who are ostracized. An apocalypse offers oppressed people an encoded word of bold assurance.

The visions reported prior to this one are primarily negative, but this final vision is purely positive. God's triumph that is promised at the end is nothing other than the completion of God's work of redemption. Yet, we should be careful to notice that redemption is not a way forward into the past, as if by forging ahead God could or would take us back to the Garden of Eden. Redemption establishes something that goes beyond all that went before. Even in the Garden when God walked with humans, God's home was not with them. Thus, current creation theologies celebrate a goodness that Revelation judges to be inadequate. The end toward which God is moving is not a mere renewal of the present creation, rather God brings forth a new cosmological context in which a new city exists that is home to both God and humanity.

The images of the vision and the words from the throne seek to speak of that which is unspeakable. What God promises is far more than a qualitatively advanced existence similar to the lives we now live. In the new creation there is no chaos, death, or despair; but life with God means more than the elimination of these negative elements of our current lives. Yet, even through vision and divine declaration John can only tell of the new promised home of God and humanity by pointing out what will not be there rather than by telling of what is there (other than God and humans). The glories of the promised triumph go beyond the words and images whereby we may comprehend. Yet, the truth of the promise is confirmed by the very word of God. The promise of God is that in the end God will make his home among humans and evil will be eliminated, but in our wildest dreams we cannot even imagine the positive dimensions of our new life with God. All the goodness our minds can conjure is finally not good enough to comprehend the glory of God's life among us. Unfortunately, to try to say more than this is to attempt to say more than Revelation is prepared to help us say. Fortunately, this is one matter in which God clearly has the final word.

The Gospel: *John 13:31-35*

Hearing the New Commandment of Christ

Setting. This lesson takes up half of the material that was treated in the lesson for Holy Thursday. Indeed, it is impossible simply to come to the lines of this lesson without some awareness of the fore-going and following portions of John. Thus, although the time that has elapsed between Holy Thursday and the Fifth Sunday of Easter is brief, the following commentary repeats a significant portion of the materials offered earlier in relation to Holy Thursday. For treatment of the foregoing material in John 13 one may return to the comments concerning the Gospel lesson for Holy Thursday.

In 13:1 John signals the move from the so-called Book of Signs (John 1–12) into the so-called Book of Glory (13–20 [21?]). Indeed, we see the supernatural significance of the time in the report concerning the activity of "the devil" in v. 2. Now, it is the day before Passover, and Jesus and his disciples take a meal together. During or after the meal Jesus washed the disciples' feet. Conversation on washing, humility, and love followed, along with Jesus' troubled prediction that Judas would betray him. Jesus dismissed Judas from the gathering, and when he had gone Jesus began to speak to the disciples. After a brief exchange with Simon Peter, Jesus eventually spoke at great length to his followers.

Structure. The initial portion of John 13 is an account of the meal and of Jesus washing the disciples' feet. Next, we find conversation, a prediction of the betrayal, and Jesus' dismissal of Judas. Then, we come in vv. 31b-35 to Jesus' initial words to his disciples, which come prior to the exchange with Peter and the lengthy "last discourses." Jesus' words to his disciples reveal the nature of his ministry and the character of Christian community. Those two themes and their relationship are the topics of the text, and they may well be the subjects of the sermon.

Significance. In the verses of the lesson, Jesus declares that his "hour" has arrived and he speaks so that we perceive the nature of the time: "Now the Son of Man has been glorified, and God has been glorified in him" (v. 31). In turn, he tells the disciples plainly that the task he leaves them is that they demonstrate to the world that they are his disciples by manifesting the same love among themselves that he embodied in washing their feet (and, even more, in dying on the cross).

Jesus' beautiful words about glorification tie together his being glorified by God and God's being glorified in him, both of which are related to Jesus' loving and exact obedience to the will of God. In other words, the glory of God was plainly displayed in Jesus Christ. What does this mean? As we see Jesus selflessly give his very life for his disciples, we see the depths of the love of God, which is indeed the substance of God's glory. Love characterizes the person of God, and for humans who are in fellowship with God, love is to characterize the life they live among themselves. Love here is not to be reduced to a sentiment or a feeling, rather it is the will to will the well-being of others at all costs to oneself. We are told that God has this capacity, and in Jesus Christ we are called to experience that love so that we ourselves become capable of embodying the same love.

Despite the beauty of this account and the poetic quality of Jesus' words, this striking lesson is a challenge for preaching. The point is at once simple and complex. The sermon should treat at least these themes: The love of God is manifested in Jesus Christ; that love is God's own glory; as Jesus' disciples we benefit from that selfless love; and as Jesus' disciples we are called to manifest that love ourselves.

The images of footwashing and the cross are appropriate for developing the proclamation. Yet, because a small minority of contemporary Christian congregations practice footwashing and because no one actually practices crucifixion today, the images will be distant and perhaps difficult for members of most churches. Thus, consultation of a full-blown critical commentary is indispensable. (R. E. Brown's commentary of John in the Anchor Bible series is a standard work.) Such study will direct the preacher to a variety of ancient texts providing vital information about footwashing and crucifixion, and this ancient literature will yield a wealth of illustrative material.

Easter 5: The Celebration

Today's visuals may be chosen to give expression to the ways in which the Church has sought to continue the work begun with Cornelius. Christian art from different cultural traditions might be exhibited around the church and on the bulletin cover. Music can be chosen to reflect the liturgical diversity that cultural diversity makes possible. The word *love,* which is central to the Gospel reading, might be reproduced in as many languages as possible.

Today's lessons provide an opportunity to consider seriously the ambiguities raised by the Gospel's call to inclusiveness and American society's preference for church membership based on like cleaving to like. In Acts we see how the Spirit demolishes the comfortable enclaves we construct for our own spiritual comfort and security. John lays the groundwork for that by rehearsing Jesus' fundamental command to love one another. He goes so far as to say that the proof of our discipleship is discerned by our ability to overcome our pride through love (remember that this occurs after the footwashing episode). The Revelation anticipates the fruition of Christ's redemptive work by the establishment of a new order of existence, which seems also to incorporate unity and diversity. God dwells with us and is the focus of our existence, but the NRSV translates Revelation 21:3 as "they will be his peoples," which suggests that differences are respected in heaven and not everyone is absorbed into a huge homogeneous mass. How is it possible to order our ecclesiastical life together so that from time to time it may seem as though a door has been opened in heaven and we glimpse the possibilities of love?

Hymns related to the theme of the new Jerusalem include: "I Want to Be Ready" (AMEC *Bicentennial Hymnal,* no. 510; *The United Methodist Hymnal,* no. 722), "Jerusalem the Golden" (AMEC, no. 478; *The Baptist Hymnal,* no. 527; *The Hymnal 1982,* no. 624; *Hymns for the Living Church,* no. 536; *Lutheran Book of Worship,* no. 347), "O Holy City, Seen of John" (*Hymnal: A Worship Book,* no. 320; *The Hymnal, 1982,* nos. 582-3; *The Presbyterian Hymnal,* no. 453; the UCC *Hymnal,* nos. 188-89; *The United Methodist Hymnal,* no. 726), and "O What Their Joy and Their Glory Must Be" (*The Hymnal 1982,* no. 623; *Lutheran Book of Worship,* no. 337; *The United Methodist Hymnal,* no. 727).

Today's intercessions may include prayers for the city of Jerusalem and a new spirit of harmony and love between those faiths that hold it sacred.

Sixth Sunday of Easter

Old Testament Texts

Acts 16:9-15 is the account of how Paul and Silas brought the gospel to Europe. Psalm 67 is either a song of thanksgiving or a petition for divine leading.

The Lesson: *Acts 16:9-15*

Staying with the Mission

Setting. The story line of the book of Acts has advanced considerably from the lesson of last week. The geographical range of the gospel, in particular, has grown larger and larger in the book of Acts. After the conversion of Cornelius by Peter in Acts 10–11, the conversion of the Gentiles is first recounted in Acts 13–14 as a mission by Paul and Barnabas. Acts 15 provides an interlude to missionary journeys by addressing problems of circumcision with regard to Gentile converts in Antioch. Paul and Barnabas remain central to the story, because they are messengers between the Jerusalem and Antioch churches. At the close of Acts 15 these central characters separate over a disagreement about whether Mark should accompany them on a new missionary journey. Barnabas takes Mark and Paul chooses Silas. Acts 16 begins "The Great Missionary Journey" of Paul and Silas. Verses 1-6 recount how Timothy joined their mission in Lystra. Geography plays an important role in interpreting Acts 16:9-15. The lectionary text has Paul in Asia on the coast of the Aegean Sea, with Greece, or more specifically, Macedonia, the next stop in his journey, located on the other side of the Aegean.

Structure. The lectionary text begins in Acts 16:9 with the account of Paul's night vision of a Macedonian person pleading for him to cross over the Aegean Sea to preach the gospel. Most commentators agree that v. 9 does not begin a new unit, but that Paul's vision is part of a larger travel section that begins in v. 6. The larger travel narrative is important for interpreting the vision, and, thus, ought to be included in the lectionary text. Acts 16:6-15 separates into two distinct stories: vv. 6-10 tell about Paul's quest for a vision and vv. 11-15 recount the story of Lydia, the first convert in Macedonia.

Significance. The two sections of the lectionary text have a different focus, which when combined complement each other.

The first half of the reading conveys a sense of frustration. Luke goes out of his way in vv. 6-10 to underscore how Paul's mission to Asia Minor consisted mainly of false starts. Twice he recounts failed attempts by Paul. First, we are told in v. 6, that Paul was "forbidden by the Holy Spirit to speak the word in Asia." Then, in v. 7, Luke tells us that even though Paul, Silas, and Timothy attempted to go into Bithynia, "the Spirit of Jesus did not allow them." The end result of this process is that this small band of zealous missionaries ends up crossing Asia Minor seemingly without enough success to warrant a story, which is no small irony, since this particular mission by Paul is often referred to as "The Great Missionary Journey." When Paul's vision in v. 9 to cross the Aegean Sea into Macedonia is interpreted within its larger literary context, it becomes clear that this vision has come into focus at some personal cost, and that it is most certainly not his first on this trip. The initial fight between Barnabas and Paul (15:36-41) and then the aborted itinerary of Paul (16:6-8) underscore how the apostle clearly had plans of his own, not all of which necessarily corresponded with God's. The key to the success of this great mission was that Paul stuck with it beyond its initial failures.

The second half of the text contrasts sharply with the first. The failed attempts at travel and mission, which resulted in a somewhat meandering path to Troas, couldn't be more different than the near perfect boat trip to Greece in one day (v. 11), and then from Neapolis to Philippi (v. 12). Note in v. 13 how third person narration ("he") gives way to first person ("we"), which suggests that perhaps Luke was also part of this group. In any case, vv. 13-15 move quickly to narrate the initial convert to Christianity in Macedonia. Lydia, a woman from the city of Thyatira, who dealt in purple cloth, was already someone who worshiped God. She heard, believed, was baptized, and, as the writer stated, "prevailed" upon the group to stay with her.

When preaching this story, accentuate the contrast between the two halves. Paul's vision to cross over the Aegean Sea into Macedonia was hardly a stained-glass experience that came to him fresh and clean one Sunday morning. Instead, it was a vision painted through a long sequence of failures that took him to the geographical edge of what he had first intended. Had he not stayed with his failures there would have been no vision. Once Luke has made that point, the second half of the text could not contrast more sharply with the first. The winds blow in the right direction and before we know it, Paul, Silas, Timothy, and Luke? are living in the home of Lydia, the first convert in Greece.

The Response: *Psalm 67*

Petition or Thanksgiving

Setting. There is debate about the form and mood of the psalm, which centers on the tense of the verbs at the beginning (v. 1) and end (vv. 6*b*, 7*a*) of the piece. They can be read as either imperfect or jussive statements, as statements of customary actions by God (God is gracious) or as petitions for certain kinds of divine action (May God be gracious). Either reading is possible.

Structure. The best way to organize Psalm 67 is to begin in the middle with v. 4, which is a call for all nations to praise God. This universal call to praise is framed with similar refrains in vv. 3 and 5 ("Let the peoples praise you, O God; let all the peoples praise you.") The beginning (vv. 1-2) and the ending (vv. 6-7) are either petitions or thanksgivings for divine blessing, with the opening verses being a recitation of the Aaronic blessing from Numbers 6:24-25.

Significance. Two aspects of Psalm 67 provide an insightful response to Acts 19:6-15. The first is the call for all nations to praise

God. This universal call for praise corresponds well with the conversion of Lydia in the Greek city of Philippi. The second important aspect of Psalm 67 as a response to Acts 19:6-15 is the insoluble form-critical confusion that is embedded within it. Is this psalm a petition, thanksgiving, or both? Such confusion provides insight into the vision of Paul to cross the Aegean Sea after several other failed attempts in his mission. His so-called Great Mission illustrates poignantly how narrow the line is between petition and thanksgiving, between asking for divine guidance and receiving visions.

New Testament Texts

The reading from Revelation presents one of the best-known and most-admired scenes from that writing, the descent of the new or heavenly Jerusalem. We learn of the hope of our direct access to God, made real and given shape through Jesus Christ. Then we learn of the glory of God that creates and sustains life in the new city, both drawing in the best of this world and leaving out all that was bad. In the Gospel lesson from John, Jesus speaks about the obedience of love, about the operation of the Spirit of truth in the life of the Christian community by bringing Christ's peace to his faithful disciples, and about his forthcoming departure (his return to his Father) and the joy it brings for those who truly love him.

The Epistle: *Revelation 21:10, 22–22:5*

Scenes from the Eschatological City of God

Setting. Readers may consult basic information about Revelation of John in the introductory remarks for the Second Sunday of Easter. The general segment of the book from which our lesson comes is a great multifaceted vision of the end that is recorded in 19:1–22:5. More specifically, our text presents parts of the scene portraying the perfected community of salvation (21:9–22:5) by telling of the descent of the new, heavenly Jerusalem and the lack of a temple in the city.

Structure. Verse 10 comes from a portion of the vision that initially describes the heavenly Jerusalem (21:9-14). Then, we completely skip the account of the measuring of the city in vv. 15-21 and come to the main part of the reading, 21:22–22:5. These verses tell of the quality of life in the new city of God. Thus, v. 10 sets up the report of the vision in vv. 22-27. The report itself opens with the dramatic line, "I saw no temple in the city," from which the following statements follow as explication. Then, in 22:1-5 one encounters the vision of the river and tree of life.

Significance. Verse 10 points to the highly symbolic nature of our reading. The high mountain should not be thought of geographically, rather the mountain recalls other biblical scenes of revelation and symbolizes the lofty nature of the ensuing sights.

The imagery of the vision is clearly derived from traditional Jewish writings and belief, but nothing could put a document more at odds with traditional Jewish piety and hope than the assertion that in God's end time there would be no temple. Historically the Temple made Jerusalem God's holy city, for it was in relation to the Temple that one recognized in a supreme way the presence of God among God's people. Moreover, the Temple made possible the drawing near of humanity to God and the Temple's cult guaranteed the very experience of God. The teachers of the Jewish faith yearned with Ezekiel 40–46 to hope for a perfected end-time temple, but what would the end time be with no temple at all?

In sharp contrast to this pattern of piety and this kind of Old Testament expectation, the vision John of Patmos reports the descent of a heavenly Jerusalem ("the" heavenly Jerusalem!) in which there is no temple at all. And, why? Because the old manner of indirect access to God through Temple and cult are made unnecessary through the direct presence of God and the Lamb in the new Jerusalem. God and the Lamb are said to be the temple of the heavenly Jerusalem. The life-giving presence of God is itself the structure and the substance of life in the new city. The vision speaks of the realization of the early Christian critique of the Temple, expressed at points by Jesus as well as his later followers.

Yet, as the report of the vision continues, we find that not only is there no temple, there is no sun or moon. Again, why? Because God's glory is the light and the Lamb is the lamp (unfortunately the alliteration is not present in the Greek!), so that the citizens of the new city live and see by the very presence of God. This new point shows that the Christian hope, which at times expressed itself in a critique of the Temple, was no pure repudiation of the hope of Israel. Careful comparison of this report about the lack of sun and moon with a statement in Isaiah 60:19-20 shows that John of Patmos' vision tells of the realization of Israel's true hope in God! Moreover, the remainder of the lines of our reading have still other clear points of contact with the eschatological expectations and hopes of Israel expressed particularly in Isaiah 60 (see especially Isaiah 60:1, 3-6, 11). We should note above all that the realized glory of God has the positive effect of drawing all the best of our world into its new reality, and we should rejoice at the promise of the exclusion of evil (vv. 24-27).

There are, however, undeniably distinctive elements in Revelation. Above all, the vision of the heavenly Jerusalem and all-providing direct presence of God are qualified by the presence of the Lamb, so that the quality of life to which one looks and for which one hopes is established by God's work in the Lord Jesus Christ whom Christians now trust and serve.

A sermon might work with the idea of "life in the presence of the Lamb." Thus, the images and ideas of worship, light, glory, salvation, and purity may be expressed in terms of the difficult, but powerfully hope inspiring, notion of the "real presence of God." The text of Isaiah 60 may well come into the development of proclamation, but Isaiah and Revelation should be appreciated for their differences as well as their similarities.

In turn, 22:1-5 introduces images illustrative of the bountiful quality of life in the very presence of God and Christ—crystal clear water, a tree with twelve fruits that bears at all times, and illuminated worshipful face-to-face life in relationship to the Lord God. The text opens by playing on images from Ezekiel 47:1-12 in vv. 1-3*a*. The heart of the vision (vv. 3*b*-5) is a dramatic declaration that salvation amounts to being in a transformed, eternal communion with God and Christ. The name of God on the foreheads of those who experience salvation shows that the saints are God's very own people. Indeed, God's brilliant clarity imparts true direction and purpose—both focused on and in relation to God's very self—to the citizens of heaven. Thus, the saints share in the glory of God's eternal rule. Bounty, identity, community, and purpose are the themes that may inform proclamation. The image-laden character of the text suggests the appropriateness of vivid, pictorial preaching.

The Gospel: *John 14:23-29*

Obedience, the Spirit, and Joy—All from Love of Christ

Setting. The general setting of the so-called Book of Signs was discussed in relation to the Gospel lesson for Holy Thursday. In this lesson, we remain in the setting of the last supper as we encounter verses from the early portion of Jesus' so-called "Last Discourse" (14:1–17:26). In the discourse Jesus speaks at length and in depth, so that we find almost every major theme of Johannine theology presented and developed. On Pentecost we shall again encounter a portion of this lesson, focusing especially on the references to the Advocate/Paraclete/Spirit in this passage. Thus, that important element of our lesson receives minimal treatment here.

Structure. The lesson presents portions of two segments (14:15-24, 25-31) of the first major section of the Last Discourse (14:1-31). Lifted from their literary context in this manner, we find that the verses of our lesson form three distinguishable sayings. First, vv. 23-24 treat the character of life as lived in and out of a relationship with God and Christ. Second, vv. 25-26 tell of the forthcoming sending of the Paraclete and how that one will teach Christ's followers. Third, vv. 27-29 pass Christ's particular peace to the disciples who are called to the steadfastness and courage of faith that brings joy. The logical flow of the material should be suggestive for the themes and the lines of proclamation.

Significance. A question from Judas (not Iscariot) in 14:22 sets up the words of Jesus in vv. 23-24, but as is so often the case in John's accounts of Jesus' exchanges with others, no direct answer is forthcoming. Rather, Jesus' answer explains (one of several times in the Fourth Gospel) what it means truly to "see" Jesus, and he continues to explain why the world cannot comprehend his self-revelation—which itself is a revelation (a self-revelation) of God! One encounters these lines and understands clearly why even the most seasoned and informed preachers quake before such texts. The statements seem to circle and loop, and while one follows their gist by noting the repetition and juxtaposition of words and phrases, the straightforward logic of the material is a challenge to track. Indeed, the gaps are as crucial as the lines uttered. Compare vv. 23-24 noting contrasts, absences or special emphases (in parentheses):

Verse 23	Verse 24
Those who love me	Whoever does not love me
will keep my word	does not keep my words
(and my Father will love them)	
(and we will come to them)	
(and make our home with them)	
	(and the word that you hear is not mine)
	(but is from the Father who sent me)

The contrast between those who do and do not love Jesus is telling. Promises are made to those who love Jesus, great and abiding promises that offer comfort and hope. The absence of equal or opposite promises is striking. No threats occur here, there is simply no offer of the presence of God and Christ in the lives of those who do not love Jesus. Moreover, in the concluding words of v. 24 we find the opposition simply set aside, as if they were absolutely unimportant, as Jesus returns to speak to those who love him. They hear the words of God through Jesus in love, whereas for those who do not love Jesus there is simply no hearing or recognition of God's will for their lives. Thus, the quality of human life and the relationship between humans and God are set in terms of the love of Jesus Christ.

As Jesus continues to speak we see that the Holy Spirit (the coming of the presence of God and the Son into the lives of believers) is the work of God among the members of the community of faith. This work means that Christ's disciples are directed ever more toward Christ himself. As lives are directed toward Christ, disciples live the life to which Christ calls us. As v. 27 makes plain, this is the experience of divine peace. Moreover, Christ's peace gives heart and courage to those who live their lives under the direction of the Advocate, the Holy Spirit, whom God sends to lead Christ's disciples in the course of their lives in the world. The parting statement in vv. 28-29 is meant as a word of comfort and encouragement, reminding Christians that they do not face life alone, for God is not indifferent, disengaged, or helpless in relation to their (our) daily lives. The supreme power of God comes to us in Jesus Christ and continues to work among us as God's Holy Spirit reminds us of the person, the teaching, and the promised coming of our Lord Jesus Christ.

While the lines of this lesson have fueled many doctrinal debates, later considerations must not dominate our reflection upon them— although we can ill afford to ignore later developments in the life of the Church. Thus, in preparation for preaching, one will find an additional commentary indispensable.

Easter 6: The Celebration

For hymns relating to the vision of the new Jerusalem, see the "Celebration" entry for last week.

Both today's epistle and Gospel readings will be familiar to some because they have heard them read so frequently at funeral services. The sermon might point out how they are therefore appropriate during Easter, since every Christian funeral is a remembrance of Christ's resurrection and a celebration of the Easter message in its own right. That explains why the Paschal candle is lit at every funeral service and every baptism, even when they occur outside of Eastertide. It is there to remind us that we have been buried and raised with Christ in baptism and that death can have no final hold over us.

The appearance of these readings may also serve to introduce the whole subject of the Christian funeral and its ability to witness to our faith. Pastors frequently lament the superficiality of local funeral customs and their inability to bring about significant change. The time of death itself is certainly inappropriate for insisting on liturgical changes that will be strange to those who are in need of the support of custom and tradition. People will be more receptive to ideas for change when they are not in a stressful condition and when they can be helped to see more clearly the ways in which the funeral service can function as their own final testimony and witness to their faith in Jesus Christ. To devote a sermon to this subject from time to time can begin to erode the force of unconsidered custom and to encourage members of the congregation to take their funeral planning seriously.

This Sunday was referred to in the Western church for many centuries as Rogation Sunday. It was a time for asking for (*rogare*, to ask) God's blessing on the fields and the spring planting. Some denominations still list it in their program calendars as Rural Life Sunday. The intercessions today may include prayers for farms and farmers and for an increased sense of stewardship for all the creation. The rogation theme is echoed in today's psalm: "The earth has yielded its increase" (Psalm 67:6a). That motto might be used in conjunction with a photo exhibit of how the earth yields its increase. Potted plants could be distributed around the building and church school classes could take responsibility for yard care and new plantings during the coming week. Such an emphasis on this day involves us with God in the whole work of creation rather than merely as receivers, which can often be the message of Thanksgiving. Hymns used only at Thanksgiving can thus be liberated to proclaim their fuller message, particularly "We Plough the Fields and Scatter." It is fitting as the offertory hymn for today.

Ascension of the Lord

Old Testament Texts

Acts 1:1-11 is the account of Jesus' ascension. Psalm 47 is a hymn celebrating the kingship of God.

The Lesson: *Acts 1:1-11*

Ascension Is an Unfinished Story

Setting. The Gospel of Luke and the book of Acts were written by the same person. This is evident in the lectionary text for this Sunday by comparing the opening words of Acts with the opening words of Luke. Each book (Luke 1:1-4 and Acts 1:1-2 or 3) begins with a prologue addressed to a certain Theophilus, who may be a person or simply a general title for the reader (Friend of God). Some of the purposes for writing this two volume work include: (1) The delay of the parousia. Why had Jesus not yet returned as early Christians had expected? (2) Closely tied to the problem of the delay of the parousia is the primary role of salvation history in Luke-Acts. Scholars debate just how Luke conceived of salvation history, but one possible configuration consists of three segments with an interim period. The first is the time of the law and the prophets from Adam to John the Baptist (Luke 16:16). The second epoch is the proclamation of the kingdom of God by Jesus, which consists of the descent of the Spirit on Jesus at his baptism (Luke 3:22) to the return of the Spirit to the Father when Jesus was on the cross (Luke 23:46). The resurrection of Jesus through the ascension of Jesus is a transitional time, before the final epoch, which consists of the proclamation of the kingdom of God by the Church. (3) The important role of the Holy Spirit both in the life of Jesus and in the ministry of the Church. And (4) the proclamation of a universal salvation to all nations. These four particular purposes all play a role in Acts 1:1-11.

Structure. Acts 1:1-11 is closely linked to the close of the Gospel of Luke. There is a thematic connection in that the Gospel ends with the ascension and the promise of the Spirit, while Acts begins with the ascension and then moves immediately to Pentecost. This thematic organization illustrates how important ascension is in Luke-Acts as a hinge for the development of a theology of the Holy Spirit. Acts 1:1-11 separates into three parts to develop the relationship of ascension and the outpouring of the Holy Spirit: vv. 1-2 are a prologue to theophany, vv. 3-8 the final address by Jesus to his disciples, and vv. 9-11 describe the ascension of Jesus.

Significance. Interpretation will focus on the final address of Jesus and the description of the ascension, in order to see how the four themes listed above have been woven into the text.

The final address by Jesus in vv. 3-8 emphasizes continuity between the teaching of Jesus before and after his resurrection. The primary message of Jesus remains the kingdom of God (v. 3). The continuity of Jesus' message even after his resurrection prompts the disciples to ask the inevitable question: Is now the time when the kingdom of God will be fully realized on earth? (v. 6). Jesus neither affirms nor denies the question. Instead he states that the temporal sequencing of the Kingdom is God's problem (v. 7). The discussion of the kingdom of God shifts focus in v. 8 to the topic of the Holy Spirit, where continuity between Jesus and his disciples is once again emphasized. The central point of Jesus is that the Holy Spirit, which has empowered the ministry of Jesus, will now empower the ministry of the disciples, but only after Jesus leaves them.

Two important conclusions for preaching arise at this point, both having implications for the relationship between Jesus and the Church. First, similar threads stitch Jesus and the Church together into one fabric. Note that the central proclamation of divine salvation, as the ushering in of the kingdom of God, remains the same through the ministry of Jesus and the Church (Acts 1:4). Another thread is the Holy Spirit, which descends from heaven to Jesus at baptism, permeates the ministry of Jesus through his resurrection and ascension, and is able to descend anew on the disciples (Acts 1:8). Second, Jesus and the Church are not identical, not from the same cloth. In fact we could probably go one step further and state that the pre- and post-resurrection Jesus are not exactly the same. These distinctions are explored in Luke by his sequencing of salvation history. Beneath the weave or web of history God moves through time and in the process God changes. The pre-baptized Jesus is not exactly the same as the the post-baptized Jesus, or the resurrected Jesus, nor are the disciples a replication of Jesus at any of these intersections. These changes are most clearly explored by Luke through the geographical organization of the two books. The Gospel of Luke is structured so that Jesus moves from Galilee to Jerusalem (Luke 9:51–24:53)—the place of his death, resurrection, and ascension. The book of Acts begins in Jerusalem with Pentecost and culminates in Rome. This structure of geography is meant to illustrate the unfolding universal claim of the kingdom of God first proclaimed in Galilee by Jesus.

The lectionary text closes with a theophany in vv. 9-11, in which Jesus is exalted as he ascends into heaven. The colorful imagery vibrates with dissonance, because, on the one hand, the storyline narrates how Jesus is leaving his disciples, while, on the other hand, the imagery of the cloud and witness describes a special manifestation of divine glory. Thus while Jesus is leaving he is simultaneously being revealed to his disciples in a special way. This conflicting imagery at the moment of ascension is important, for it reinforces the web of the two points noted above, how there is both continuity and difference between Jesus and the disciples. The continuity between Jesus and his disciples is both one of overlapping identity in that each will be filled with the Holy Spirit, and of mission, in that each must proclaim the kingdom of God in ever widening circles. The difference between Jesus and the Church is underscored through the exaltation of Jesus symbolized through his theophanic ascension. Jesus is not the disciples, he ascends to heaven in a cloud.

The Ascension is not the first time that Jesus has been distinguished from his disciples through theophanic imagery, it has been

151

used earlier by Luke to describe the Transfiguration of Jesus in 9:28-36. Both accounts emphasize the cloud as a sign of exaltation (for Old Testament examples see Exodus 24:12-18 or 40:35-36), and in each there are two witnesses to provide commentary (Moses and Elijah at the Transfiguration and two divine beings in white robes at the Ascension). Their commentary illustrates how these two stories must be read together and how, when they are, the emphasis of each is not on the present event, but on the next manifestation of Jesus' glory. In the story of the Transfiguration, only Luke provides the content of the conversation between Jesus and Moses and Elijah, when he tells us in 9:31 that they were discussing the Ascension. This unique insertion of commentary suggests that the point of the Transfiguration for Luke is not on the event itself but on its power to direct the disciples to the future event of the Ascension. The same dynamic is at work in Acts 1:9-11. Even though the Ascension is a fulfillment of the Transfiguration, the commentary of the two witnesses in v. 11 suggests that, like the Transfiguration, the emphasis is not to provide a conclusion to the Transfiguration but to reveal the future return of Jesus ("This Jesus, who has been taken up from you into heaven, will come in the same way as you saw him go into heaven."). The ascension of Jesus locks the Church into God's movement into the future, which will inevitably culminate in the return of Jesus and the complete realization of the kingdom of God. But being locked into God's movement into the future is hardly the end of a story. Thus the Ascension is merely a transition, an unfinished story of how the Church sometimes travels with God, and other times splits off onto its own track. The parousia is when there will only be one track.

The Response: *Psalm 47*

A Hymn of Praise

Setting. Psalm 47 is an imperatival hymn (note the command in v. 1, Clap!, or in v. 6 Sing!), which celebrates the kingship of God. This rule is conceived as an exultation, hence the link back to the theophanic imagery of exaltation in the ascension of Jesus.

Structure. The psalm divides into two parts: vv. 1-5 and 6-9. Each section begins with an imperatival call for praise (vv. 1 and 6), and each section then follows with reasons why God should be praised (vv. 2-5 and 6-9). Note how these sections both begin with the word "for" (Hebrew, *ki*), which is the expected form for hymns.

Significance. Psalm 47 celebrates the enthronement of God in the Temple through the imagery of universal rule. Note the recurring motif of how God rules "over all the earth" (v. 2), how God "is the king of all the earth" (v. 7), and how God "is king over the nations." This rule emanates from the Temple, "God sits on his holy throne" (v. 8). Although the account of Jesus' ascension certainly picks up the imagery of exaltation, the force of Psalm 47, with its more imminent imagery of an enthroned God, pushed the reader of Acts 1:1-11 to envision not simply the ascension but also parousia of Jesus.

New Testament Texts

The text from Ephesians is a grand expression of thanksgiving that recognizes and celebrates God's saving power in Jesus Christ. The lesson from Luke is one of two texts telling of the ascension of Jesus (the other is Acts 1:1-11, especially 1:9). Ephesians actually meditates on the exaltation of Christ into power in the heavenly places, whereas Luke recalls the Ascension per se which he certainly understands to be the means or the manner of Jesus' being borne into heaven.

The Epistle: *Ephesians 1:15-23*

Thanking God for the Riches We Have in Christ

Setting. Normally Pauline letters open with a greeting, as Ephesians does in 1:1-2, and then follows a prayerful thanksgiving prior to the beginning of the body of the letter. Ephesians, however, has a blessing of God for the blessings Christians have received (similar to a Jewish *berakah*) in 1:3-14; and then, 1:15-23 is the usual thanksgiving prayer report.

Structure. There are two broad, related movements in the lesson:

First, in vv. 15-19, hearing of the believers' faith in the Lord Jesus and of their love of the saints, Ephesians

- gives thanks for the believers and
- asks that God may give the believers a spirit of wisdom and revelation resulting in the knowledge of God
  - for their illumination unto hope (part of God's call)
  - for an awareness of their inheritance among the saints
  - for an appreciation of God's great saving power.

Then, Ephesians shifts the focus in vv. 20-23 to comment on God's mighty working in Jesus Christ. Thus, the meditation takes a christological turn, both remembering and declaring

- God's resurrection of Christ,
- God's exaltation of Christ over
  - all powers and places,
  - all names in all times, and
- God's making Christ the head of his body, the church, which now shares the benefits of his glory.

Significance. These lines from the thanksgiving of the letter (1:15-18) unpack the meaning of God's blessings for us as believers and members of the Church. The prayer asks that God give the believers the gift of intimate comprehension of God. Such understanding is not knowledge that comes through human ingenuity or effort—such as knowledge that comes from studying a math textbook. Rather, Ephesians asks for the gift of God's self-disclosure, which would come as an ever deepening relationship between God and the believers. This kind of knowledge is charismatic and mysterious and comes as God works in our lives, not as we grasp after unseen things. In relation to God, the life of believers is characterized by the joy of hope and an awareness of the richness of God's grace. Believers have a new attitude, but it is not the result of positive thinking; it comes purely as a gift from God, and it activates a new way of living. Verse 19 makes this clear by speaking of "the immeasurable greatness of his power for us" and of "the working of his great power."

With this mention of God's magnificent power, the thanksgiving takes a christological turn to illustrate the clearest testimony to God's power—namely, the resurrection of Christ. As is normal in New Testament thought, Ephesians refers to the resurrection as something that God did. Though Christology articulates and illustrates the truths of God, God never takes the backseat to Jesus Christ. This manner of thinking is the pattern of early Christian reflection, and from time to time we have to remind ourselves that the glory of divine radiance emanates from God, lest we lose sight by blocking God out with a "Son umbrella." As we meditate on Christ, we ponder the greatness of God.

The passage continues by recalling the range of Christian conviction in relation to Christ, speaking of his exaltation, his power over all other powers, and his relationship to the Church, which participates in his majesty. As the first mention of God's power in v. 19 stated that it was/is "for us," so now in v. 22 we read that God "has put all things under [Christ's] feet and has made him the head over all things for the church." In this christological mediation, which ultimately celebrates the powerful work of God, there is a deep conviction that what God has been about in Christ has profound significance for the Church. This idea often causes discomfort for Christian theologians living and working in comfortable settings, for the passage seems "triumphalistic" or "self-aggrandizing." But we have always to recall that these lines were most likely composed when Christians did not have any worldly power and, in fact, were facing opposition and persecution. Far from celebrating current power and status, these lines are a critical statement of faith about God's grace and generosity that would sustain believers in difficult circumstances. We should avoid using these lines to excuse our tendency toward living in luxury.

The Gospel: *Luke 24:44-53*

Celebrating the Ascension of the Lord

Setting. The Gospel of Luke portrays the raised Jesus coming to his disciples on the evening of Easter in Jerusalem. Luke tells of Jesus' mysterious, even disturbing, appearance. But by recalling both Jesus' words about the reality of his crucified body and Jesus'

155

eating in front of the disciples, Luke makes sure the reader knows that this event was neither an apparition, a hallucination, nor the appearance of a ghost.

With the reality of the raised Jesus' presence established, Luke recalls Jesus' final teaching and instructions to the disciples. Then, Luke concludes the Gospel with a brief account of the Ascension and a note about the subsequent joy of the disciples.

Structure. Three pieces of tradition make up the verses of our lesson. First, vv. 44-49 record Jesus' teaching concerning the meaning of his death and resurrection, his commissioning of the disciples as witnesses (compare Matthew 28:16-20 and Acts 1:8), and his promise of the forthcoming outpouring of the Holy Spirit on the disciples (see Acts 1:8 and 2:1-13). This material is loosely connected with the second and third items in the lesson which are intricately related to each other. Second, vv. 50-51 offer a remarkably brief account of the Ascension; and third, vv. 52-53 report how the disciples returned to Jerusalem with great joy and devoted themselves to praising God in the Temple.

This cluster of information informs the reader of Luke that the joy of the Christian community was the result of God's resurrection and exaltation of the crucified Jesus. Moreover, the joy is an anticipation of the power of the Holy Spirit that will be endowed upon the disciples, which itself empowers them to bear witness to God's saving work in Jesus Christ.

Significance. Interpreters struggle in comparing the lines of our lesson with Luke's parallel account in Acts 1:1-11. Recent literary-critical analysis of both passages finds the Gospel account of Jesus' ascension to be more an implicit reference than an explicit depiction as found in Acts. Such a distinction helps to get past the obvious differences between the accounts to reflect upon Luke's theological concerns in handling this traditional material.

In connecting vv. 44-49 with the two pieces focused on the Ascension (vv. 50-51, 52-53) the lectionary wisely directs us to the substance of the joyous celebration of the Ascension of the Lord. Thus, we see the references to the law, the prophets, and the Psalms and we recall the words of Jesus throughout Luke in reference to his "fate." The explicit concern with the scriptures alludes especially to the lines of the Emmaus road story (24:47) and to the fuller exposition of the Old Testament materials presented in some detail in the speeches throughout Acts. Thus, Jesus' own interpretation of scripture is shown to be the key to Christian exposition of the Old Testament in relation to Jesus. What is striking here is the penultimate position given to the biblical materials. Jesus gives the "true" meaning to scripture as he himself is the key to the interpretation of the text. One starts with a concern and commitment to Jesus Christ and then turns to the Bible, so that scripture is a holy tool, not an ultimate sacred object demanding direct allegiance. We worship a living Lord to whom we relate in faith with the assistance of Scripture.

In turn, the reference to Jesus' suffering, death, and resurrection indicates plainly that God works through these events for salvation. And, salvation is understood to be universally available forgiveness of sins. As God confronts humanity in the person of Jesus Christ—through his life, death, and resurrection—we see plainly the ultimate power of God. We are told that (not how) God has acted in Jesus Christ for the benefit of all humankind. Jesus' life, death, and resurrection are proclaimed as the demonstration of God's own love and concern for us!

Then, Jesus commissions the disciples to be his witnesses. The blessing of the forgiveness of sins means a call to ministry. But as Jesus explains, the ministry to which we are called is not our task alone, for witness takes place in the power of God's Holy Spirit. Thus the forgiveness that we experience and the same forgiveness that we are called to proclaim come to us, by the power of God, as simultaneous gift and task.

In preaching the Ascension we proclaim and celebrate the supreme power of God as known through Jesus Christ. The larger Gospel lesson informs us of the saving character of God's power, the necessity of bearing witness to God's work in Jesus Christ, and the assurance of the presence and leadership of God's Holy Spirit for the faithful execution of our commission.

Ascension Day: The Celebration

The lessons for today may be used in place of those for the following Sunday, the Seventh Sunday of Easter, since few congregations may be expected to have a special service on Ascension Day.

Preachers frequently seem a little embarrassed and apologetic about preaching on the Ascension. Forty days earlier they stood in the pulpit and declared, "Christ is risen!" Now they appear to have doubts as to just how high! The problem may have to do with the Lukan chronology that separates (as John does not) a unified Paschal event into identifiable actions: Resurrection, Ascension, and Empowerment. The problem may also have to do with a scientific worldview that we may feel compels us to explain the Ascension in a way that we avoid when preaching about the impact of the Resurrection. We appear either to be confused about what happened to the body or condescending about the lack of a sophistication on the part of our congregations which (we think) keeps them from understanding the problem. The Ascension may provide no better time to talk about the difference between the New Testament's cosmology and ours and what is involved in trying to understand its imagery with our points of reference. Surely we preachers are only deceiving ourselves if we think the issue has never occurred to our hearers! An honest presentation of the question may be liberating to many and open the way to authentic biblical faith unimpeded by the necessity of having first to subscribe to a first-century view of the universe.

Karl Barth suggested that what changes about Christ in the mystery of the Ascension is simply the place, the vantage point, from which he operates. He moves from a human place to a divine place without ceasing to be human, just as he did not cease to be divine in his human place. To concentrate on the direction of the movement in a spatial sense is to miss the point. This movement places our humanity in the presence of divinity; it is a glorification not only of Christ, but of all human nature. Political systems argue for human dignity from many perspectives. Christianity demands human dignity not because of any rights we may believe ourselves to have, but because our worth is derived from that humanity that is a part of the Godhead. The exaltation of the incarnate Christ, says Barth, "refutes all attempts at setting up another government, another 'place,' from where orders and promises reach us. It is the ultimate refutation of all dictatorships" (*The Faith of the Church* [London: Collins, 1960], p. 98).

The following collect joins together themes from the Ephesians reading and the Ascension narratives. Notice that its emphasis is on Christ's ascension not as the beginning of a "real absence," but as the occasion for Christ's general availability:

> Almighty God, whose blessed Son our Savior Jesus Christ ascended far above all heavens that he might fill all things: Mercifully give us faith to perceive that, according to his promise, he abides with his Church on earth, even to the end of the ages; through Jesus Christ our Lord.
>
> (Book of Common Prayer, p. 226)

Hymns particularly appropriate for the Ascension are:
   Alleluia! Sing to Jesus
   All Hail the Power of Jesus Name
   And Have the Bright Immensities
   Crown Him With Many Crowns
   Hail the Day That Sees Him Rise
   Hail, Thou Once Despised Jesus
   The Head That Once Was Crowned with Thorns

Seventh Sunday of Easter

Old Testament Texts

Acts 16:16-34 continues the account of Paul and Silas in Philippi that began with the conversion of Lydia. Psalm 97 is an enthronement psalm.

The Lesson: *Acts 16:16-34*

The Power of the Gospel in Philippi

Setting. Philippi is the first setting of Paul's missionary journey in Greece (Acts 16:11-40), which will eventually include Thessalonica (Acts 17:1-9), Beroea (Acts 17:10-15), Athens (Acts 17:16-33), and Corinth (Acts 18:1-17). Luke has structured Paul's activities in Philippi into three events, which are associated with three different people. First, there is the conversion of Lydia, an independent businesswoman who was already a believer in God before Paul's arrival (vv. 11-15). Second there is the exorcism of a slave girl (vv. 16-18), which lands Paul and Silas in jail (vv. 19-24). And, finally, there is the conversion of the jailer (vv. 25-34). These three events provide archetypes of how the power of the gospel is conveyed.

Structure. The lectionary text includes the final two activities of Paul in Philippi: the exorcism of the slave girl in vv. 16-18, and the conversion of the jailer in vv. 25-34. The two events are linked with the scene of Paul's and Silas's arrest in vv. 19-24.

Significance. Luke explores the power of the gospel from three different perspectives in recounting Paul's activity in Philippi. Each of these perspectives requires a brief summary even though the lectionary is focused on the final two.

The opening story of Lydia in vv. 11-15 is fairly typical of the missionary genre. Upon arrival in Philippi, Paul, Silas, Timothy, and possibly Luke (note the first person "we" in the narrative) seek out a place of worship on the Sabbath. They find such a place on the outskirts of the city, join the worshipers, and eventually Paul preaches the gospel of Jesus. Lydia is persuaded of the truth of the gospel, but Luke phrases her acceptance differently in v. 14: "The Lord opened her heart to listen eagerly to what was said by Paul." Acceptance leads to baptism, which results in generosity when Lydia invites the group to stay in her house.

The second story in vv. 16-18 departs radically from the first. It is not a story about the proclamation of the Gospel with the intent to persuade. Rather it begins as a confrontation, or perhaps better as an annoyance, between the spirit possessed slave girl and the group of missionaries. The spirit possessed slave girl follows the group and without invitation or consent proclaims in v. 17, "These men are slaves of the Most High God, who proclaims to you a way of salvation." This action continues for several days until Paul, out of frustration commands the spirit in the name of Jesus to leave the girl, which it immediately does. This is not a story about conversion. We hear nothing of the slave girl after the exorcism, except that she could no longer make money for her owner. Further, Luke gives the reader no basis for interpreting Paul's action as anything other than annoyance. The point of this story is less about the slave girl than it is about the spirit within her. The confrontation between Paul and the spirit is similar to that of Jesus and the unclean spirit in the man at the Capernaum synagogue in Luke 4:31-37. Each story includes a confrontation in which the spirit states a basic truth about God, which is treated as a confrontation that results in the silencing of the spirit. At the very least the confrontation underscores how the spirit or kingdom of God is let loose in Greece. And, as is frequently the case in the Gospels, it is the spirit world that initially makes note of the fact.

The third story returns to the topic of conversion in vv. 25-34, but it is very different from the account of Lydia. The confrontation between Paul and the unclean spirit underscored how the presence of the missionaries in Philippi introduced a cosmological conflict into

Greece. Yet, spiritual conflicts always have political implications, as was suggested by the slave girl's comment that the missionaries were, themselves, slaves to the Most High God. The subversive character of this recognition about the missionary's ultimate allegiance is played out momentarily when Paul and Silas are arrested for disturbing the peace and breaking Roman law, which lands them in jail. Prison becomes the setting for the second conversion in Philippi, this time not of a God-fearer, but of a (most likely) retired Roman soldier. This conversion is not the direct result of Paul's persuasive preaching. Instead the more cosmological dimension of the story retains center stage. There is an earthquake (one of the classic signals of divine theophany in the Old Testament), which miraculously opens the doors of the prison and loosens everyone's chains. The jailer sees the open doors and, knowing his fate, attempts to commit suicide, at which time Paul informs him that no one had left, which then prompts his response of trembling (an appropriate reaction to theophany in both the Old and New Testaments). As Hans Conzelmann notes in his *Commentary on the Acts of the Apostles,* this is a miraculous story that leaves many questions unanswered: "How did Paul, in the inner prison, know that the jailer was about to kill himself? How did he know that all the prisoners were still there? How did his cry reach the jailer? How did the jailer know for which prisoners the miracle had taken place?" The point of this story is to underscore the miraculous nature of the event as something that cannot help prompting the jailer to seek salvation (v. 30). The proclamation of the gospel then follows leading to baptism, which results in hospitality.

Luke's sequencing of the events in Philippi is certainly not arbitrary, and the communication of this sequence could very well provide the basis for preaching. The chapter allows us to see the spread of the gospel into Greece in all of its dimensions, including two kinds of converts, as well as the spiritual and political confrontation that is implied in being a slave to God rather than the state. The gospel moves (1) from the God-fearer Lydia (2) to a cosmological confrontation between God and spiritual powers on the one hand and a social confrontation between the disciples and political powers on the other hand. This confrontation provides the matrix for a further spread of the gospel, this time (3) to someone who knows nothing about God. A common theme throughout the chapter is that it is God and not the disciples who are spreading the gospel in these very different contexts, opening the heart of Lydia (v. 14), casting out the spirit (in the name of Jesus, v. 18), and finally bringing the jailer to conversion through a theophanic earthquake (v. 30).

The Response: *Psalm 97*

The Enthronement of God and the Gift of Righteousness

Setting. Psalm 97 is one of the Enthronement Psalms. This group of psalms includes 47, 93, 96, 97, 99 and is characterized by the proclamation, "Yahweh is King!" Psalm 97 celebrates the enthronement of God in the Temple, which from a theological perspective is a celebration of divine imminence. When the psalm is read as a response to Acts 19:16-34 it takes on a subversive quality, since it is such a confession that prompted the exorcism of the slave girl bringing Paul and Silas into direct conflict with the Roman empire.

Structure. Psalm 97 separates into four parts. It begins in vv. 1-2 with a description of the enthronement of God in the Temple. Verses 3-6 describe this enthronement with the traditional imagery of theophany (e.g., clouds, darkness, fire, lightning, and the reaction of fear by nature—mountains, earth, heavens—and by people). Verses 7-9 outline the effects of God's appearing (shame and gladness). Finally, vv. 10-12 describe the relationship between God and the righteous.

Significance. Psalm 97 is a celebration of the presence of God within the worshiping community. The setting of worship underscores two points. First, the place of the theophany is not in the world but in worship (vv. 1-7). And, second, that it is only within the context of worship that the relationship between God and the faithful ones is established (vv. 8-10). In fact, commentators define the "righteous ones" in vv. 11-12 solely by means of worship. The righteous are those who are allowed to enter the sanctuary where God has been enthroned. Thus there is an inner connection between being in the sanctuary when God is enthroned and being righteous. This conception of righteousness goes against our modern understanding of the term, which tends to be more ethical—namely, that being righteous means acting in a certain reasonable way which may not necessarily require revelation. Righteousness in Psalm 97 is not first and foremost about action, rather it is more sacramental. It is a revelatory quality that accompanies God in the act of being enthroned ("righteousness and justice are the foundation of his throne," v. 2*b*). This quality, then, is transferred to those who are present. This means that the effect of theophany in the context of worship is the divine gift of righteousness. This transformation in character forces the worshiper back into the larger world as an ethical agent of God's, because the goal of the divine enthronement is for "all the peoples [to] behold his glory" (v. 6*b*). Acts 16:11-34 provides several illustrations of how this process works.

New Testament Texts

Both texts are a challenge for preachers, largely because they are abstract and encoded with language that proves cryptic for contemporary readers. Revelation concludes with a parting word of grace that is designed to fill the readers with daring trust in the Lord. In John, Jesus prays for his followers—especially those who will believe through the preaching of his disciples—and he expresses concern for the faithfulness and unity of the church. Both passages show that the Lord Jesus continues to work among the members of the church for the accomplishment of God's purposes.

The Epistle: *Revelation 22:12-14, 16-17, 20-21*

Christ's Promised Blessing

Setting. The book of Revelation comes to a conclusion in 22:6-21. The ending is quite deliberate in form and content. Comparison of the language and content of these lines with the opening verses of the writing (especially 1:1-3) reveals that the conclusion emphasizes the purpose and goal of the entire book. Thus, the unity of Revelation is underscored, despite the clear sections and diverse literary genres that make up the whole.

Moreover, this purposeful ending has clear positive and negative dimensions. On the one hand, it offers encouragement, hope, and direction to those members of the early church to which Revelation is addressed. But, on the other hand, it denounces and warns those not aligned with the members of the church; these persons are portrayed as degenerates who are set against God's revealed will. By omitting vv. 15, 18-19 from the reading the lectionary discards the overt negative elements. Yet, since it is unlikely that non-Christians would have read Revelation with its rich apocalyptic symbolism and its inferior Greek, we should probably understand that even the denunciations and warnings were included for the benefit of Christian readers. If so, the omission suggested by the lectionary does not seriously alter the sense or purpose of the passage, although if the lines that are deleted are handled with sensitivity they do not necessarily lead to railing against non-Christians in preaching.

Structure. Our reading comes from three of four sections composing the conclusion of the book. Verses 12-16 are a confirmation of the message of Revelation by Jesus himself speaking through his messenger, the angel, to John. Then, vv. 17-20 are a combination of liturgical declarations (vv. 17, 20) and warnings (vv. 18-19). The last verse of the reading, v. 21, is also the last verse of the book, and it has the form of an epistolary benediction; thus, it concludes both the final section of the work and the book as a whole.

The themes of the reading are the majesty of the Lord Jesus Christ, the blessing of those faithful to him, the hope of the coming of the Lord, the call of the faithful to the blessing of eternal life, and the grace of the Lord Jesus Christ. One should notice how in this material the focus shifts three times back and forth from the person and the power of the Lord to the meaning of the Lord's person and power as blessing for the faithful.

Significance. From the content and the structure of the lines of the reading we can see clearly that the aim of this conclusion to Revelation is to invigorate the hope of believers by recalling the person, the power, and the promise of the coming of the Lord Jesus Christ. The coming of Christ is a blessing for the Church because, as Revelation declares explicitly and implicitly (both ways occur in this reading), Christ comes to pronounce God's judgment upon "everyone's work."

In executing God's final and ultimate judgment, the reading tells us that the Lord Jesus Christ shares the very characteristics of God: he is Alpha and Omega, the bright morning star whose appearance brings on the great Day of the Lord. As the one who comes in God's judgment, the Lord Jesus is the hope of the Church. For those who turn to the Lord and commit themselves fully to him, judgment means blessing. Jesus comes bringing his reward with him, so that the Spirit and the bride (the Church) call for his coming with eager anticipation. The degree of the commitment of those who hope for the coming of Christ is seen in the imagery of v. 14, which recalls vividly Revelation 7:14. The idea of washing robes implies absolute commitment, and in Revelation this image probably refers to the suffering of martyrdom in faithfulness to Christ. For those who actually give their lives for the Lord, the promise of these verses is the blessing of "the water of life as a gift." Above all, our reading tells us that the relationship of faith established between the Lord Jesus Christ and the members of the Church is a relationship that rests secure in the person, the power, and the promise of the Lord; so that whatever pressure or persecution believers face, the final judgment is the Lord's. Thus, the relationship is secure and ultimately above the forces of opposition.

The message of this reading is one of hope. The hope itself is secured by the Lord, not by human actions. That point is one that proves perennially hard to comprehend. Moreover, for persons in oppression the text will speak clearly, but for those not suffering persecution this passage may prove hard to hear. If the preacher faces an affluent or comfortable congregation, he or she must strive to make the hearers conscious of the hardships endured by others. Indeed, perhaps the most difficult part of this text to grasp is the universal or cosmic scope of the vision inherent in these verses (and the rest of Revelation). The good news of hope because of the grace of the Lord Jesus Christ is gospel for all the Church. The words of Jesus—revealing his person, power, and promises—are directed toward all Christians as we stand together. The message of Christ is not to be reduced to personal piety (although personal piety is important, and our text has crucial implications for us as individuals). Our Lord is Lord of all, and he calls us into a new existence that transforms our relationship to him and, in turn, to one another.

The Gospel: *John 17:20-26*

Christ's Own Prayer for the Future

Setting. Recognizing the general context in which these verses occur, Jesus' Last Discourse, is crucial for grasping the importance of the lesson. After Jesus and the disciples came to their last meal together and after Jesus had washed the disciples' feet, he began to speak at great length (chapters 14–17), delivering what some scholars refer to as his "last will and testament." Jesus' words are not those of a dead man, however; rather they inform the disciples (and the readers of John!) in detail of the identity and intentions of the crucified, risen, and exalted Lord. Jesus' speaking shifts at the beginning of John 17 from teaching to prayer, although the prayer itself is "instructive." Our lesson is the last section of Jesus' prayer. As he prays to his Father for the benefit of his disciples, he prays beyond the present and into the future for those who will come to believe in him through the preaching of the disciples themselves.

Structure. The content and form of these six verses is remarkably complex. While the lesson is very coherent, still we may view distinct elements in the lesson. The point of Jesus' prayer is made in v. 20. Then, in vv. 21-23 we find a highly patterned statement wherein five poetic phrases in vv. 21-22*a* are repeated with slight variation in vv. 22*b*-23:

1.	21*a*	that they may all be one
	22*b*	so that they may be one
2.	21*b*	As you, Father, are in me and I am in you
	22*c*	as we are one
3.	21*c*	may they also be in us
	23*a-b*	I in them and you in me, that they may be completely one
4.	21*d*	so that the world may believe that you have sent me
	23*c*	so that the world may know that you have sent me
5.	22*a*	the glory that you have given me I have given them
	23*d*	and [that you] have loved them even as you have loved me.

In turn, v. 24 states Jesus' desire for those who believe in him to be with him; and vv. 25-26 tell of Jesus' past, present, and future revelation to his disciples and recognize that there ultimately is no separation from divine love for those who believe.

Significance. Despite their poetic beauty (or, perhaps because of it), these lines at the conclusion of Jesus' prayer are open to interpretive debate. Clearly the prayer is for those who will come to faith and membership in the Church after the time of Jesus' earthly ministry, and clearly Jesus' prayer states a concern for the unity of these believers. Moreover, it is clear that the model for the unity of the believers is the oneness of the Father and the Son, and Jesus' prayer recognizes that the unity for which he prays comes through divine will and action, that is, it is not a human achievement. Finally, it is clear that the unity for which Jesus prays is characterized by love. Nevertheless, even when we recognize these elements of the prayer, we are far from absolute comprehension of Jesus' petition. What does it mean to believe in Jesus? What, in fact, is the unity for which he prays? What does it mean to love?

Belief, unity, and love are crucial but vague Christian concepts. We often move from one to the other of these topics using one term to define the other, thus erecting a facade of pious terminology that still has little precision. Coming to terms with these less than absolutely clear issues may point the way to preaching this passage. First, belief in the Fourth Gospel is always focused in relation to Jesus Christ (3:16-18). More precisely, true belief in Jesus Christ means perceiving and confessing something of the vital, even unique, relationship between him and God (9:33; 12:44-45). Belief also has consequences—those who believe in Jesus Christ as God's Son do the work which Jesus himself did in the name of his Father (9:4; 14:12).

Second, the issue of unity is more difficult. While we see from John 10:16 that unity is more than the harmony of a single congregation, the larger story of the Johannine community and the larger corpus of Johannine literature make it equally clear that unity is not thought of on a scale such as that envisioned in today's international, interdenominational ecumenical discussion. Yet, we do see that unity has both vertical and horizontal dimensions—that is, it means divine-human relations and human-human relationships. All

unity is the result of God's power. And the explanation of the consequences of unity in v. 21 ("so that the world may believe that you
have sent me") shows that unity has a vivid evangelistic purpose.

Third, we come to love. Perhaps only in tennis and the Fourth
Gospel can we really be certain what this word means. Jesus commands those who believe in him to love one another (13:34). He
gives himself as the standard of that love (13:34), stating plainly that
love means to will the well-being of others to the degree that one
would give one's own life for the benefit of the others (15:13). Such
love serves as a testimony to "the world" concerning Jesus Christ
(17:23). Thus, we see that belief, unity, and love are related; but the
relationship has a definite content, form, and purpose.

Easter 7: The Celebration

Although Easter Day is now seven weeks in the past, it is important
to remember that we are still celebrating Easter, and that the lessons
for the day call for interpretation in light of the Paschal mystery.

The lesson from Acts, combining as it does the exorcism of the slave
girl and the conversion of the jailer, should call attention to the centrality of Jesus Christ as the source of Paul's power rather than invite curi-
ous inquiry about the private lives of the girl and the jailer. Notice the
observation in the above commentary that the slave girl is healed
because of Paul's irritation over being hounded and interrupted, and
nothing is said about her conversion. It is not only the jailer who comes
to faith, but he brings with him his household, and on the face of it they
appear to have little to say about the matter. These facts suggest that
the preacher should not be tempted into some facile and romantic
explication of conversion that lays greater emphasis on our belief than
on the power of the risen Christ to bring us to belief.

Revelation 22:17 may serve as today's call to worship, either
responsively or with a solo voice. Notice that the reference to the
Spirit anticipates next Sunday's celebration of Pentecost on the one
hand and on the other reminds us that in our worship we are recalling the events of salvation history rather than reproducing them.

The use of the *Marana tha* ("Our Lord, come" = I Corinthians
16:22) also occurs in one of the most ancient Christian prayers, the

grace after meat in the Didache. The following adaptation of it could be used in today's service before the final blessing. Notice also that the unity theme from the Gospel lesson is reflected here.

We thank you, holy Father [God],
for your sacred name
which you have lodged in our hearts,
and for the knowledge and faith and immortality
that you have revealed through Jesus, your child.

To you be glory for ever.

Almighty Master,
you have created everything
for the sake of your name,
and have given everyone food and drink to enjoy
so that they offer you thanks.
But to us you have given spiritual food and drink
and eternal life through Jesus, your child.
Above all, we thank you that you are mighty.

To you be glory for ever.

Remember, Lord, your Church,
to save it from all evil
and to make it perfect by your love.
Make it holy,
and gather it together from the four winds
into the holy city which you have prepared.

For yours is the power and the glory for ever.

Let grace come and the world pass away!

Hosanna to the God of David!

Those who are holy, come. Those who are not, repent.

Marana tha!

Our Lord, come!

Amen.

(Adapted from Cyril C. Richardson, ed., *Early Christian Fathers* [Philadelphia: Westminster, 1953], pp. 175-76)

The hymn, "O Morning Star, How Fair and Bright," is usually associated with the Epiphany and the Sundays following, but the lessons make it particularly appropriate today. See *The Lutheran Book of Worship*, no. 76; *The Presbyterian Hymnal*, no. 69; *The Hymnal* (UCC), no. 112; and *The United Methodist Hymnal*, no. 247. The Lutheran version's six stanzas can allow for a lot of variation in how the hymn is shared by the congregation (choir, solo voices, men, women, etc.). The translation in the Episcopalian book, *The Hymnal 1982,* does not relate well to today's lessons and should not be used.

Pentecost

Old Testament Texts

Acts 2:1-21 is the account of Pentecost. Psalm 104:24-34, 35*b* is a hymn celebrating the power of God in creation.

The Lesson: *Acts 2:1-21*

Pentecost

Setting. It is important to notice the setting of the entire Pentecost story in the overall structure of Acts. In Acts 1 we moved from Easter up to Pentecost, seeing the risen Lord present among the disciples, instructing them and promising the coming of the Holy Spirit. Acts 2 narrates the fulfillment of Jesus' promise, and it shows us quite dramatically what the disciples do as a result of being anointed with the Spirit—they are transformed from being mere eyewitnesses to being genuine ministers of the word. The remainder of Acts, beginning in Acts 3, tells how certain faithful disciples continue the Christ-ordained and Spirit-empowered mission.

Structure. There are three distinct sections in this lesson: vv. 1-13, vv. 14-16, and vv. 17-21. Verses 1-13 have three subsections, which provide a narrative introduction to Peter's speech in 2:14-40. First, we learn of the time and place (2:1) and, second, vv. 2-4 tell of the coming of the Holy Spirit upon the disciples. Third, vv. 5-13 introduce the assembly of "devout Jews from every nation" and tell of the mixed reaction of the crowd to the disciples. Verses 14-16 provide the setting for Pentecost in Jerusalem, before describing the events of Pentecost—the divine anointing of believers, the ensuing miracle(s), and the misunderstanding of the masses. Verses 17-21 correlate the events of Pentecost with Old Testament prophecy.

172

Significance. Peter's claim is that prophecy is fulfilled in the Pentecost, and he identifies divine activity and the presence of the Holy Spirit with the effects on the believers. This allows him to name the time as "the Last Days." In turn, this naming of the time indicates the crucial nature of the Pentecost event as a moment of cosmic crisis and divine judgment. The outcome of the eschatological fulfillment of prohecy at Pentecost is that humans will call on the name of the Lord for salvation.

Notice the boldness of Peter's speech at Pentecost. He makes several points clear in this speech, and at least two prominent points are inherent in this week's lesson: (1) Only those in a postive relationship to Jesus Christ—as the one in whom God's plan was/is fulfilled—are in a position to understand properly the present work of God. The masses could not comprehend the effects of the Holy Spirit on the believers, because they had no knowledge of the promise of the risen Jesus that the Spirit would come upon the disciples. The superior knowledge of the disciples is not a source of privilege, but a call to service in behalf of Christ to the masses. Christianity is not Gnosticism. Whatever we know by the grace of God is given to us in order to direct us to ministry. (2) Christians have a peculiar perspective on time: it is the Last Days—a penultimate time of fulfillment, judgment, and salvation. An important dimension of the ministry to which we are called is the naming of the times. Time, from the Christian point of view, is not a spiral, or a circle, or even a mere line. Time belongs to God, who changed it in the life, death, resurrection, and ascension of Jesus Christ and the subsequent outpouring of the Holy Spirit. Pentecost means that the time of God's promise (a future time) has been brought to fulfillment (made present). In the current moment, described in the lesson as "the Last Days," we live under the claim of God. This declaration of Peter means that the future time for which humanity had hoped has, in fact, already broken into history so that things are no longer the same (which is signified by the miraculous events of Pentecost). Thus there is a certain sense in which the past (prophetic promises), present (outpouring of the Holy Spirit), and future (the Last Days) interract as a single time in the event of Pentecost. Pentecost is simultaneously a fulfillment of past divine promises and a taste of the end of time wrapped up in the present, and it is this twist of time that gives rise to Christian ministry. This peculiar fact of time is the content of the gospel.

The Response: *Psalm 104:24-34, 35*b

Celebrating God's Creative Power

Setting. Psalm 104 is a hymn celebrating the creative power of God. As such it shows a connection to Genesis 1 in vv. 6 and 25 as well as to creation motifs from other cultures in the Ancient Near East. Verses 19-24 have a marked resemblance to the Egyptian hymn of Akhenaton (*Amenophis IV*), especially with the encyclopedic listing of aspects of creation. In addition references to primeval waters in vv. 6 and 26 also suggest the influence of flood mythology that was current among Assyrians and Canaanites.

Structure. The lectionary reading included only the later portion of Psalm 104. Two problems in structure arise with the given text. First, there is a question of whether v. 24 is an introduction to what follows as the lectionary reading would indicate, or a summary to the preceding section of vv. 19-24. Second, the invective against evil in v. 35*a* has been left off. The function of the invective in v. 35*a* is that it pulls the psalmist's meditation on creation back into the moral sphere, which is absent if the reading ends at v. 34. With these two problems as background the lectionary text can be outlined as follows:

> I. Praise of God as Creator (vv. 24-30)
>> A. Work (v. 24)
>> B. Leviathan (vv. 25-26)
>> C. Summary (vv. 27-30)
> II. Concluding Praise (vv. 31-34)
>> A. Call for continued theophany (vv. 31-32)
>> B. Promise to praise (vv. 33-34)
>> C. Closing praise (35*b*)

Significance. Psalm 104 provides a glimpse of the end time or last days that are described by Peter, through the description of God's power throughout creation. The psalm also carries a view of time in which the present reality and future ideal touch. On the one hand the Spirit of God is let loose in creation (v. 30*a*), yet, on the other hand, the creative power of God is an ongoing process that requires the continual attention of God (v. 30*b*).

New Testament Texts

Pentecost is obviously the time for reflection upon the coming of the power of the Holy Spirit upon the Church. Paul ponders the Spirit's reformation of life as the cause for Christian hope, and in John, Jesus speaks about the operation of the Spirit of truth in the life of the Christian community, which brings the peace of Christ to his faithful disciples. The parameters for both texts as suggested by the lectionary create problems for interpretation, for we are asked to focus on snippets or sound bytes which drop out of the logical flow of much larger sections of text. Thus, in what follows the reflections run past the boundaries of the lessons to offering information that makes the lectionary passages intelligible.

The Epistle: *Romans 8:14-17*

The Implications of Life in the Spirit

Setting. In Romans Paul wrote to a congregation he had not founded and which he had never visited. Thus, he laid out the main lines of the gospel he preached in more careful detail than in any of his other preserved correspondences. Romans 5–8 is a major part of Paul's presentation. In turn, within the larger section of Romans 5–8 the eighth chapter is itself a nearly self-contained unit with clearly identifiable parts. Generally this chapter is a meditation on the nature and significance of Christian life. It is crucial to notice two items. First, this section "ends" Paul's long reflection on the operation of grace in chapters 5–8. Second, this beautiful, hopeful meditation immediately precedes the following agonizing section of Romans, chapters 9–11, which wrestles with the fate of the disbelieving portion of Israel in the working of God's grace.

Structure. Chapter 8 is neatly structured. Verses 1-11 take up the theme of Christian life as life in the Spirit. Then, vv. 12-17 employ the metaphors of sonship (obscured in the NRSV) and childhood (preserved and amplified to take in sonship) to reflect upon the significance of our relationship to God. Next, vv. 18-30 bring a strong eschatological cast to Paul's thought by speaking of future freedom and glory. Finally, vv. 31-39 conclude this section declaring the ulti-

PENTECOST

mate destiny of Christian life to be victory through "the love of God
in Christ Jesus our Lord." Beginning the lesson with v. 14 is not
ideal, as is clear from the first word of v. 14, "For," which refers to
and builds on the statement in vv. 12-13. Dropping back and including those verses in the reading will set the context of the contrast of
flesh/Spirit upon which vv. 14-17 build; and since we come to this
reading from Romans on Pentecost without the benefit of a sustained study of the epistle, some consideration of Paul's ensuing
remarks is in order, if not absolutely necessary.

Significance. Following Paul closely through the careful sections of
chapter 8, especially vv. 14-17 (or, 12-17), is not easy work. Even the
initial words in v. 12, "So then," tell us that Paul is drawing conclusions from the previous verses where he made the clear positive point
that Christian life is life in the Spirit, not life in the flesh or under the
law of sin. Verses 12-17 give the "because" for vv. 1-11. To paraphrase: Christian life is life in the Spirit because persons led by the
Spirit are the children of God. In one way Paul is speaking about
Christian identity or self-understanding (more communal than individual, though there are implications for individuals); but he goes on to
speak about the significance of such life. Life in the Spirit is much
more than an identity, indeed it is a relationship to God that has come
as a gift from God. For now, the distance between (sinful) humanity
and (righteous) God is overcome as God adopts us as God's children.
And Paul continues. Since we are now God's children, we will be
heirs. This expansion of the metaphor accomplishes at least two
things: (1) It introduces a profound eschatological cast to the meditation—we are experiencing grace, and there is more to come! (2) It
translates Christian suffering into meaningful suffering. If we are co-
heirs with Christ, Paul says our suffering for Christ (he is not talking
about routine health or financial problems) is like Christ's own suffering—that is, an anticipation of the glory to which God will bring us.

Unfortunately the thoughts begun in vv. 12-17 are left dangling
without consideration of the extension and development of Paul's
ideas in vv. 18-30; thus, the following remarks: Having registered
the motifs of life, the Spirit, relationship to God, eschatology, Christ,
and suffering before the Romans, Paul advances his argument by
shifting subjects slightly. His topic becomes life in the Spirit as a life

176

of hope. Paul focused on the Christian community in vv. 1-17; then, those remarks become a springboard to the declaration of Paul's vision of the cosmic scope of the operation of grace through the work of the Spirit. Paul's line of reasoning is difficult, because we are not adept at thinking in such cosmic terms, nor are we really accustomed to reflecting upon the need of creation for redemption. Yet, the apostle works with a deep conviction that the very fabric of creation is itself, like humankind, captive to the corrupting power of sin, so that creation, or the cosmos, is at odds with God; but Paul also believes and states that "the creation itself will be set free from its bondage to decay and will obtain the freedom of the glory of the children of God." In Paul's vision of God's work of redemption, humanity, and the cosmos are intricately related to one another. The fate of the one is the fate of the other. Why? Because humanity and the cosmos have in common that they are creatures, created by the one creator God. The hope of all creation is in the faithful creator who did not abandon a sin-trapped creation but in Jesus Christ reclaimed and thoroughly identified with all of creation. Thus, Paul can make the bold statement found in Romans 8.

The Gospel: *John 14:8-17 (25-27)*

Jesus, His Father, Disciples, and the Holy Spirit!

Setting. The general setting of the so-called Book of Signs was discussed in relation to the Gospel lesson for Holy Thursday. In this lesson for Pentecost, we return to the early portion of the section of the Book of Signs known as the "Last Discourse" (14:1–17:26). Jesus speaks here in such a way that we encounter the presentation and development of almost every major theme of Johannine theology, but we are concerned on Pentecost with the particular portion of the Last Discourse that forms our lesson primarily because of the references to the Advocate/Paraclete/Spirit in these verses.

Structure. We encountered a portion of this lesson on the Sixth Sunday of Easter, but the new complement of verses gives the lesson a particular sense for Pentecost. The lesson comprises portions of three distinct segments (14:1-14, 15-24, 25-31) of the first major section of the Last Discourse (14:1-31). When the verses placed in parentheses in the lectionary are included in the lesson, we find that our lesson is made up of five sayings that are linked together like pearls on a string. First, in vv. 8-11 Philip poses a question that allows Jesus to speak explicitly about his and "the Father's" oneness. Second, vv. 12-14 proclaim the ongoing work of God, seen in Jesus himself, and carried forth by Jesus' disciples after his return to the Father. Third, vv. 15-17 qualify the love of the disciples for Christ by referring to their keeping his commandment; and, in turn, Jesus promises his obedient disciples the comfort, guidance, and presence of the Spirit after his departure. Fourth, vv. 25-26 clarify the nature of the work of the Spirit among the disciples. Fifth, v. 27 is actually the opening lines of a segment running from v. 27 through v. 31, but coming at the end of the lesson it forms a benediction in which Christ pronounces his peace upon his disciples. The several themes of this lesson may form a cluster of topics for proclamation, or any one or more subunits may be selected for Pentecost proclamation. If less than all the suggested verses are used, one should certainly take up the lines that refer to the Spirit (vv. 15-17, 25-26).

Significance. Jesus speaks of his return to the Father and calls his disciples to unswerving faith in him in the opening verses of John 14. As the story is told, at least Philip did not find Jesus' words easy to follow—and any reader of the Last Discourse cannot help being sympathetic with Philip! The question Philip poses solicits a statement from Jesus about his divinity—oneness with the Father—and the knowledge of God that is available to those who believe in Jesus Christ. Then, Jesus' next remarks inform us that faith in Christ provides more than mere illumination, it empowers those who believe. Lest we falsely conclude that it is the knowledge of God itself that gives us power in faith (a rather Gnostic understanding), read vv. 12-14 carefully and notice that it is through our relationship to Christ himself, through prayer, that Christ himself works through us as we relate to him in faith.

With this foundational understanding, the lines of the Last Discourse go on to speak of the active nature of discipleship, but again with the clear recognition that the work of Christ that is done by his disciples is, in fact, defined and empowered by God. As we relate to Christ faithfully, obeying his commandments, we are assured of

Christ's faithfulness to us in his promise of the gift of the Spirit. The reality of a faith relationship to Christ is marked out and made real by the indwelling of the Spirit in the lives of persons of faith. Verses 15-17 are not a call to "follow the rules" so that you will get a great reward. The commandments of Christ are, above all, a call to mutual love among Christ's disciples that expresses the reality of the loving relationship between our Lord and ourselves.

As Jesus continues to speak we see clearly a point implicit in the foregoing verses—namely, that the gift of the Holy Spirit is not the inheritance of a powerful tool that we manipulate. As the Holy Spirit works among the members of the community of faith, Christ's disciples are directed ever more toward Christ himself. This activity of the Holy Spirit is a freeing from the paralyzing preoccupation with self and even one's immediate community. As lives are directed toward Christ, disciples live the life to which Christ calls us. As v. 27 makes plain, this is the experience of divine peace, which is more than the absence of strife; Christ's peace is the active well-being of those who relate to him in faith. Indeed, Christ's peace gives heart and courage to those who live their lives under the direction of the Advocate, the Holy Spirit, whom God sends to lead Christ's disciples in the course of their lives in the world.

Pentecost: The Celebration

Today concludes the celebration of the Great Fifty Days, the time of the Church's period of intense meditation upon the meaning of the Resurrection, Ascension, and empowerment by the Spirit. It is important not to historicize the day, as though we are reenacting the original event. Pentecost is not a rupture in the Christian year; it is the consequence of the Resurrection. Jesus makes clear in today's Gospel lesson that the Advocate is his gift to the Church, so that we are not left destitute of the presence of Christ. The Resurrection is an ongoing experience in the Church's life because of the presence of the Spirit in our midst reminding us of all that Christ has said and done. Charles Wesley, in one of his hymns, refers to the Holy Spirit as "the remembrancer." It would serve today as a bridge between the readings from Romans and John.

1. Come, thou everlasting Spirit,
   bring to every thankful mind
   all the Savior's dying merit,
   all his sufferings for mankind. [love for humankind]
2. True recorder of his passion,
   now the living faith impart,
   now reveal his great salvation,
   preach his gospel to our heart.
3. Come, thou witness of his dying;
   come, remembrancer divine,
   let us feel thy power, applying
   Christ to every soul, and mine.

Suggested tunes are Cross of Jesus, Galilee, Kingdom (For the Bread), and Stuttgart.

St. Irenaeus commented on the promise of the Advocate in the following way:

> This was why the Lord had promised to send the Advocate: he was to prepare us an offering to God. Like dry flour, which cannot become one lump of dough, one loaf of bread, without moisture, we who are many could not become one in Christ Jesus without the water that comes down from heaven. And like parched ground, which yields no harvest unless it receives moisture, we who were once like a waterless tree could never have lived and borne fruit without this abundant rainfall from above. Through the baptism that liberates us from change and decay we have become one in body; through the Spirit we have become one in soul. . . .
>
> If we are not to be scorched and made unfruitful, we need the dew of God. Since we have our accuser, we need an Advocate as well. And so the Lord in his pity for man, who had fallen into the hands of brigands, having himself bound up his wounds and left for his care two coins bearing the royal image, entrusted him to the Holy Spirit. Now, through the Spirit, the image and inscription of the Father and the Son have been given to us, and it is our duty to use the coin committed to our charge and make it yield a rich profit for the Lord.
> (*Christian Prayer: The Liturgy of the Hours* [Baltimore: Helicon Press, 1976], pp. 1793-94)

For other comments and suggestions relevant to the liturgical celebration of Pentecost, the reader should consult the entries in the appropriate volumes in this series for Years A and B.

Scripture Index

Old Testament

New Testament

A Comparison of Major Lectionaries

YEAR C: ASH WEDNESDAY THROUGH THE DAY OF PENTECOST

	First Lesson	Psalm	Epistle	Gospel
		ASH WEDNESDAY		
RCL	Joel 2:1-2, 12-17	51:1-17	II Cor. 5:20b–6:10	Matt. 6:1-6, 16-21
RoCath	Joel 2:12-18	51:3-6, 12-14, 17	II Cor. 5:20–6:2	Matt. 6:1-6, 16-18
Episcopal		103		
Lutheran	Joel 2:12-19	51:1-13	II Cor. 5:20b–6:2	
		THE FIRST SUNDAY IN LENT		
RCL	Deut. 26:1-11	91:1-2, 9-16	Rom. 10:8b-13	Luke 4:1-13
RoCath	Deut. 26:4-10	91:1-2, 10-15	Rom. 10:8-13	
Episcopal	Deut. 26:(1-4) 5-11	91	Rom. 10:(5-8a)8b-13	
Lutheran	Deut. 26:5-10	91		

	First Lesson	Psalm	Epistle	Gospel
THE SECOND SUNDAY IN LENT				
RCL	Gen. 15:1-12, 17-18	27	Phil. 3:17–4:1	Luke 13:31-35
RoCath	Gen. 15:5-12, 17-18	27:1, 7-9, 13-14		Luke 9:28-36
Episcopal				Luke 13:(22-30) 31-35
Lutheran	Jer. 26:8-15	42:1-7, 11-15		
THE THIRD SUNDAY IN LENT				
RCL	Isa. 55:1-9	63:1-8	I Cor. 10:1-13	Luke 13:1-9
RoCath	Exod. 3:1-8, 13-15	103:1-4, 6-8, 11	I Cor. 10:1-6, 10-12	
Episcopal	Exod. 3:1-15	103		
Lutheran	Exod. 3:1-8b, 10-15	126		
THE FOURTH SUNDAY IN LENT				
RCL	Josh. 5:9-12	32	II Cor. 5:16-21	Luke 15:1-3, 11b-32
RoCath	Josh. (4:19-24); 5:9-12	34:2-7	II Cor. 5:17-21	
Episcopal		34	II Cor. 5:17-21	Luke 15:11-32
Lutheran	Isa. 12:1-6		I Cor. 1:18-31	

	First Lesson	Psalm	Epistle	Gospel
THE FIFTH SUNDAY IN LENT				
RCL	Isa. 43:16-21	126	Phil. 3:4b-14	John 12:1-8
RoCath			Phil. 3:8-14	John 8:1-11
Episcopal			Phil. 3:8-14	Luke 20:9-19
Lutheran		28:1-3, 7-11	Phil. 3:8-14	Luke 20:9-19
THE SIXTH SUNDAY IN LENT: PASSION/PALM SUNDAY				
RCL	Isa. 50:4-9a	31:9-16	Phil. 2:5-11	Luke 22:14–23:56
RoCath	Isa. 50:4-7	22:8-9, 17-20, 23-24	Phil. 2:6-11	
Episcopal	Isa. 45:21-25, or Isa. 52:13–53:12	22:1-21		Luke (22:39-71); 23:1-49 (50-56)
Lutheran	Deut. 32:36-39	31:1-5, 9-16		Luke 22:1–23:56

	First Lesson	Psalm	Epistle	Gospel
HOLY (MAUNDY) THURSDAY				
RCL	Exod. 12:1-4 (5-10), 11-14	116:1-2, 12-19	I Cor. 11:23-26	John 13:1-7, 31b-35
RoCath	Exod. 12:1-8, 11-14	116:12-13, 15-18		John 13:1-15
Episcopal	Exod. 12:1-14a	78:14-20, 23-25	I Cor. 11:23-26 (27-32)	John 13:1-15 or Luke 22:14-30
Lutheran	Jer. 31:31-34	116:10-17	Heb. 10:15-39	Luke 22:7-20
EASTER DAY				
RCL	Acts 10:34-43	118:1-2, 14-24	I Cor. 15:19-26	Luke 24:1-12
RoCath	Acts 10:34, 37-43	118:1-2, 16-17, 22-23	Col. 3:1-4 or I Cor. 5:6-8	John 20:1-9
Episcopal		118:14-29	Col. 3:1-4	Luke 24:1-10
Lutheran	Exod. 15:1-11	118:1-2, 15-24	I Cor. 15:1-11	Luke 24:1-11 or John 20:1-9 (10-18)

	First Lesson	Psalm	Epistle	Gospel
THE SECOND SUNDAY OF EASTER				
RCL	Acts 5:27-32	118:14-29 or 150	Rev. 1:4-8	John 20:19-31
RoCath	Acts 5:12-16	118:2-4, 13-15, 22-24	Rev. 1:9-13, 17-19	
Episcopal	Acts 5:12a, 17-22, 25-29	111 or 118:19-24	Rev. 1:(1-8) 9-19	
Lutheran	Acts 5:12, 17-32	149	Rev. 1:4-18	
THE THIRD SUNDAY OF EASTER				
RCL	Acts 9:1-6 (7-20)	30	Rev. 5:11-14	John 21:1-19
RoCath	Acts 5:27-32, 40-41	30:2, 4-6, 11-13		
Episcopal	Acts 9:1-19a	33	Rev. 5:6-14	John 21:1-14
Lutheran	Acts 9:1-20			John 21:1-14
THE FOURTH SUNDAY OF EASTER				
RCL	Acts 9:36-43	23	Rev. 7:9-17	John 10:22-30
RoCath	Acts 13:14, 43-52	100:1-3, 5	Rev. 7:9, 14-17	John 10:27-30
Episcopal	Acts 13:15-16, 26-33 (34-39)	100		
Lutheran	Acts 13:15-16a, 26-33	23		

	First Lesson	Psalm	Epistle	Gospel
		THE FIFTH SUNDAY OF EASTER		
RCL	Acts 11:1-18	148	Rev. 21:1-6	John 13:31-35
RoCath	Acts 14:21-27	145:8-13	Rev. 21:1-5	
Episcopal	Acts 13:44-52	145	Rev. 19:1, 4-9	
Lutheran	Acts 13:44-52	145:1-13	Rev. 21:1-5	
		THE SIXTH SUNDAY OF EASTER		
RCL	Acts 16:9-15	67	Rev. 21:10, 22–22:5	John 14:23-29
RoCath	Acts 15:1-2, 22-29	67:2-3, 5-6, 8	Rev. 21:10-14, 22-23	
Episcopal	Acts 14:8-18		Rev. 21:22–22:5	
Lutheran	Acts 14:8-18		Rev. 21:10-14, 22-23	
		ASCENSION DAY		
RCL	Acts 1:1-11	47	Eph. 1:15-23	Luke 24:44-53
RoCath		47:2-3, 6-9	Eph. 1:17-23	Luke 24:46-53
Episcopal				Luke 24:49-53
Lutheran		110	Eph. 1:16-23	

190

	First Lesson	Psalm	Epistle	Gospel
THE SEVENTH SUNDAY OF EASTER				
RCL	Acts 16:16-34	97	Rev. 22:12-14, 16-17, 20-21	John 17:20-26
RoCath	Acts 7:55-60	97:1-2, 6-7, 9	Rev. 22:12-14, 16-17, 20	
Episcopal		68:1-20 or 47	Rev. 22:12-14, 16-17, 20	
Lutheran	Acts 16:6-10	47	Rev. 22:12-17, 20	
THE DAY OF PENTECOST				
RCL	Acts 2:1-21	104:24-34, 35b	Rom. 8:14-17	John 14:8-17 (25-27)
RoCath	Acts 2:1-11	104:1, 24, 29-31, 34	I Cor. 12:3-7, 12-13	John 20:19-23
Episcopal	Acts 2:1-11	104:25-37	I Cor. 12:4-13	John 20:19-23 or 14:8-17
Lutheran	Gen. 11:1-9	104:25-34	Acts 2:1-21	John 15:26-27; 16:4b-11

A Liturgical Calendar

Ash Wednesday Through
The Day of Pentecost 1993–2001

	1993 A	1994 B	1995 C	1996 A	1997 B
Ash Wed.	Feb. 24	Feb. 16	Mar. 1	Feb. 21	Feb. 12
Lent 1	Feb. 28	Feb. 20	Mar. 5	Feb. 25	Feb. 16
Lent 2	Mar. 7	Feb. 27	Mar. 12	Mar. 3	Feb. 23
Lent 3	Mar. 14	Mar. 6	Mar. 19	Mar. 10	Mar.2
Lent 4	Mar. 21	Mar. 13	Mar. 26	Mar. 17	Mar. 9
Lent 5	Mar. 28	Mar. 20	Apr. 2	Mar. 24	Mar. 16
Passion Sun.	Apr. 4	Mar. 27	Apr. 9	Mar. 31	Mar. 23
Holy Thur.	Apr. 8	Mar. 31	Apr. 13	Apr. 4	Mar. 27
Good Fri.	Apr. 9	Apr. 1	Apr. 14	Apr. 5	Mar. 28
Easter Day	Apr. 11	Apr. 3	Apr. 16	Apr. 7	Mar. 30
Easter 2	Apr. 18	Apr. 10	Apr. 23	Apr. 14	Apr. 6
Easter 3	Apr. 25	Apr. 17	Apr. 30	Apr. 21	Apr. 13
Easter 4	May 2	Apr. 24	May 7	Apr. 28	Apr. 20
Easter 5	May 9	May 1	May 14	May 5	Apr. 27
Easter 6	May 16	May 8	May 21	May 12	May 4
Ascension Day	May 20	May 12	May 25	May 16	May 8
Easter 7	May 23	may 15	May 28	May 19	May 11
Pentecost	May 30	May 22	June 4	May 26	May 18

	1998	1999	2000	2001
	C	A	B	C
Ash Wed.	Feb. 25	Feb. 17	Mar. 8	Feb. 28
Lent 1	Mar.1	Feb. 21	Mar. 12	Feb. 4
Lent 2	Mar. 8	Feb. 28	Mar. 19	Mar. 11
Lent 3	Mar. 15	Mar. 7	Mar. 26	Mar. 18
Lent 4	Mar. 22	Mar. 14	Apr. 2	Mar. 25
Lent 5	Mar. 29	Mar. 21	Apr. 9	Apr. 1
Passion Sunday	Apr. 5	Mar. 28	Apr. 16	Apr. 8
Holy Thur.	Apr. 9	Apr. 1	Apr. 20	Apr. 12
Good Fri.	Apr. 10	Apr. 2	Apr. 21	Apr. 13
Easter Day	Apr. 12	Apr. 4	Apr. 23	Apr. 15
Easter 2	Apr. 19	Apr. 11	Apr. 30	Apr. 22
Easter 3	Apr. 26	Apr. 18	May 7	Apr. 29
Easter 4	May 3	Apr. 25	May 14	May 6
Easter 5	May 10	May 2	May 21	May 13
Easter 6	May 17	May 9	May 28	May 20
Ascension Day	May 21	May 13	June 1	May 24
Easter 7	May 24	May 16	June 4	May 27
Pentecost	May 31	May 23	June 11	June 3